THE GREEN CASANOVA

For Marion

dinas

The
Green Casanova

Mike Bloxsome

An Affectionate Biography
of Peter Freeman, Maverick MP

"A remarkable book…
about a brilliant humanitarian and devolutionist."
— **Rhodri Morgan, First Minister of the Welsh Assembly**

"A hero of the Newport tradition of radical creative dissent.
A great book!" — **Paul Flynn, MP**

Published in association with Newport Chartist Publishing

Cover illustration © Western Mail & Echo

ISBN: 0 86243 741 5

Printed and published in Wales
by Y Lolfa Cyf., Talybont, Ceredigion SY24 5AP
e-mail ylolfa@ylolfa.com
website www.ylolfa.com
tel. (01970) 832 304
fax 832 782
isdn 832 813

Acknowledgements

I would like to thank the following, most sincerely. Paul Flynn – Peter's successor as a Newport MP – for advice, encouragement, and so much more. The late John Marsh and the late Ivy Hughes for their reminiscences. Peter Clark for introducing me to the research establishments of London – except the House of Commons library, where Helen Holden was kind enough to look up documents on my behalf. David Mander, whose writings told me about the London where Peter grew up. The honorary secretaries in Peter's constituencies, who compiled the minutes I have quoted from. Also, Dave Marsland of the Theosophical Society in Wales; Chris Reed of the RSPCA; and Ann Kelly, who translated my correspondence with the authorities in Vienna. Bernard Jones and Tom Rees, who both read my first draft, most carefully. For the final editing, it has been a pleasure to work with Dafydd Saer of Y Lolfa. Lastly, there's David Mayer, who not only advised me about illustrations, but taught me how to use a computer, very patiently. Everyone else I ought to thank is part of the story.

Mike Bloxsome, 2004

Foreword

Peter Freeman raced like a shooting star across the parliamentary firmament trailing a dazzling aurora. His trajectory was sometimes capricious but always defined by originality, conviction and idealism. Peter was a backbenchers' backbencher untouched by the tyranny of the party whips, electoral pressure or the media. Assertive, intelligent, principled and unambitious for office, he was the living nightmare for party disciplinarians. Many contemporary backbenchers have been castrated, mesmerised and lobotomised by ambition. The legacies of their careers will not be celestial, trails not of stars but slugs.

Newport was a hospitable habitat for Peter the vegetarian after the sneering, doltish abuse heaped on him by the local aristocracy – the 'county set' – in his previous rural parliamentary seat. Newport Labour Party annually renews its pride in its Chartist roots and rededicates itself to progressive causes. It was a delicious pleasure to remind Tony Blair of the city's radical independence. On the day after he appointed the new Archbishop of Canterbury, there was a meeting of the Parliamentary Labour Party. Tony was taken aback when I told him that the new Archbishop had always been a reliable supporter of all Labour Party Policies, adding "as interpreted by Newport West Labour Party". In his distinguished 11-year-stint in the city Rowan Williams echoed and built on the courage and originality of the Chartists and Peter Freeman.

Mike Bloxsome reveals in this fascinating book that Freeman's vision was two generations before his time. He tried to ban fox hunting with dogs three quarters of a century before the Commons were convinced. The animal rights movement has not yet caught up with the strength and purity of the conviction that forced him to embrace a cruel death for himself.

To the dim-witted, Peter's conduct and views seemed random and contradictory: a rampant womaniser who was moved to a self-sacrificial tender lifelong devotion; the successful entrepreneur who planned to reshape the worker-employer relationship; the impassioned internationalist who longed for a Welsh parliament; the prophetic social reformer who was an adherent of a church that has almost vanished; the world class sportsman who refused life-improving medicine because of its origins. All were facets of a coherent unique political personality. Mike Bloxsome has captured the living memories of this archetypal environmentalist at the precise moment when they were about to disappear into oblivion. Posterity should now grant Peter Freeman's memory the respect, gratitude and admiration denied to him during his tumultuous, extraordinary and ultimately tragic life. *The Green Casanova* presents the world environmental movement with a new hero!

Paul Flynn MP

Chapter 1

By Way of Introduction

PEOPLE SAY TO ME, 'Why bother about someone as obscure as Peter Freeman?'

Well, obscure he might have been, but boring he undoubtedly wasn't. No-one that I know of would disagree with me here. Certainly not the old men who as young men were his political associates in Wales; or the old ladies, in Wales and far beyond, who were the objects of his desire when young and pretty, because my subject was an accomplished philanderer. He was also an advocate of women's liberation; an important industrialist; an animal rights activist, much to the embarrassment of his respectable friends; and a Welsh Open tennis champion in both the Men's Singles and – more appropriately, given his amorous personal history – the Mixed Doubles. Nor was that all. He was a Penarth local councillor who might have gone to prison for his activities as a committee chairman – though not for corruption, I hasten to add, or anything else dishonourable. So it was only to be expected that he, an Englishman, would sit in parliament as a Welsh MP, becoming something of a Welsh nationalist into the bargain, and a Green Campaigner, too – long before the term was ever invented.

This was the picture that emerged as I worked my way through the archives of various public libraries – newspapers, mostly, bound together in hefty six-monthly volumes. But there were private archives, too: in cardboard boxes; in supermarket carrier bags; or neatly stacked on shelves. What I liked best, however, were the conversations I had with Peter's family and friends (enemies, too) beginning with the occasion when the telephone rang while I was doing the washing-up after dinner.

'Nicholas Freeman,' said a self-assured voice at the other end of the line, what you might call an upper-class voice. But amiable, not snobbish at all.

A couple of weeks earlier, I had rung the Freeman cigar factory in Cardiff, which Peter had managed before he first became an MP in 1929. 'No, sorry,' they said. 'There aren't any Freemans left here any more. They were taken over by Gallagher's in Surrey. So why not try them?'

They didn't have any Freemans, either; none at all. But the marketing manager happened to know Nicholas, who was in the business of importing cigars. Very expensive ones.

'I'm Peter's great-nephew,' said Nicholas on the phone, 'and I'm told you want to pick my brains, what there is of them.'

This was just the first of many contacts with members of the Freeman family. But it was a particularly poignant one, because he didn't have long to live, as I discovered a few months later when a friend of mine sent me an obituary of him from the *Daily Telegraph* (for August 4th, 2000). Although he didn't tell me he was dying, there was something about the way he asked me what Peter had died of, and what age he was, which made me say to my wife as soon as I'd put the phone down that I thought he might have cancer like his uncle.

Nicholas wasn't exactly an admirer of Peter, describing him as a 'crank' for being – amongst other things – a vegetarian.

'He wouldn't be considered so eccentric now,' I said. 'He was way ahead of his time,' which seemed to please him. Then he asked me how I'd first got to know of his unusual uncle, a story which pleased him so much that he might even have been tempted to modify the word 'crank'. But not quite, for reasons which will be apparent a little later.

I first heard of Peter in Cardiff after the war, in the house of a boy called Tommy Farquharson whom I was at school with, whose father – also Tommy – had kept goal for Cardiff City when they won the FA Cup in 1927. Tommy senior had long been retired from football, and now ran a small tobacco shop. He obtained his cigars from the Freeman factory, where he'd sometimes kicked a ball around with 'Mr Freeman, the former manager,' as he called him. 'He was good, too,' he said, 'and could have been a professional, even an international, if he hadn't been sidetracked into politics.'

When Nicholas was asking me about his great uncle's death, I told him that he had refused to have morphine for the terrible pain he had endured, on the grounds that it had been developed by 'cruel experiments on helpless animals'.

'Did he, by God!' he said. And it was the feeling he put into those words, as much as anything else, which made me suspect that Nicholas was himself a very sick man.

In the *Daily Telegraph* obituary, it said he imported his cigars mainly from Cuba, and that he had raised about £1.5 million for medical aid in Havana. He did this by holding a series of auctions in Claridge's Hotel, where every single item under the hammer – wielded by Nicholas himself – was a box of cigars that had been autographed by his fellow smoker, Fidel Castro.

What a man that Nicholas was! Being a Tory of the old school and a member of all the right clubs in London – the MCC, White's, etc – didn't stop him from collaborating with a Communist dictator to raise money for a worthy cause, even when that cause was in the dictator's own country.

Not long after I spoke to him, Nicholas hired the Spanish Finance Minister's yacht, together with its crew, and set sail for the Caribbean to spend his last ever birthday there – his 62nd – in the company of his family.

He told me that Peter's name wasn't really Peter, but Bernard William. Or Bernhard William, rather – including that foreign-looking 'h' – as I found out when I sent for a copy of the birth certificate in order to check what Nicholas had said. Another thing he told me was that his uncle had taken the name Peter because he was convinced that a Second Coming of Christ was imminent. And equally convinced that he, Peter, would fulfil the same role in modern times that his adopted namesake had fulfilled in the Holy Land a couple of thousand years earlier – of closest companion and Chief Apostle to the Saviour of Mankind.

Now, what was I to make of that?

Here was my hero, all normal one minute – kicking a ball around in a factory yard, while no doubt casting an appreciative eye on any of the office or workshop girls who happened to be passing by – and all mystical the next, thinking of himself as God's trusted lieutenant, with a message for the entire human race.

How could they possibly co-exist, these two such contradictory aspects of the same character? And there was a third one as well – at odds with the mysticism, if not the athleticism. He could, in addition, be as logical as the next man when necessary. But Peter wasn't unique; not in the context of his early manhood at the start of the 20th. century – when the conflict over Darwin was as bitter as ever, and astronomy was supporting evolution by allowing it much more time to go from amoeba to man than the paltry few thousand years it had been allotted in the Bible.

People were confused by it all, including many eminent people. They teetered on an intellectual tightrope, you might say – between new logic and ancient mysticism, science and religion. There was Sir James Jeans, for example – a mathematical physicist at Cambridge – who worked on the origins of the solar system and on star formation, looking everywhere for natural causes. But he also believed that God was at the back of these natural causes, referring to Him as a supreme mathematician. Like himself, in fact. Only not so academic; more hands-on. And there was Sir Oliver Lodge, Professor of Physics at Liverpool and designer of the British electricity supply system, the National Grid. They don't come more rational than that. Now do they? Or more down to earth. And yet he also maintained that it was possible to make contact with the dead, publishing a book about it, too – *The Reality Of The Spiritual World*.

All the same, believing yourself to be a chief assistant to the Son of God – and changing your name accordingly – is more than a bit extreme. Even by the standards of other mystics.

Had Nicholas got it wrong, then? Or his informant, I should say; the elderly relative whom he went to see – on my behalf – in the middle of his preparations for that last-ever birthday in the Caribbean. How kind this was! And, apparently, how typical! He didn't even tell me he was going; just went, and then wrote to me, admitting that the relative was over 90 and 'a little confused'. But a confused informant can, unfortunately, still be right. (And I say 'unfortunately' because I didn't want him to be).

Trying to find out whether there was any truth at all in this elderly relative's Chief Apostle theory – as reported to me by Nicholas – took a very long time, during which I became quite fond of the Peter Freeman who actually walked this earth, or crawled it at first; the sixth of nine brothers and sisters, who were brought up for at least part of their lives in 'a flat above a factory', as one of them later described it.

He was born on October 19th, 1888, at Hoxton, one of the most deprived areas in all of London. An unlikely place of origin for a future man of wealth, living off his investments, though not for a mystic, or a sportsman, or a Casanova, or the Labour MP of radical inclinations which he also became.

Chapter 2

Fetching Up that Boy

YOU COULDN'T FIND a better guide to the Hoxton of Peter's childhood than Charles Booth, a shipping magnate turned social investigator, who called it 'the leading criminal quarter of London, and indeed of all England'. Other observers said that its tenement houses were 'rat infested' and 'fronted by mud, filth and garbage'. Inside, they were said to 'stink'. It's no wonder that rents were difficult to collect, especially as drink was the chief means of escape from these conditions; together with the annual migration down to Kent for picking hops on the farms. The whole family would go – grandparents, cousins and babies, aunts and uncles, the lot. And they would earn enough for the fathers amongst them to enjoy their evenings in the pub, while economising on food and clothing for their wives and children.

All of these problems are reflected in the songs they sang, like 'Don't Go Out Tonight, Dear Father!' written in 1886, a couple of years before Peter was born, and another, more macabre one referring to public executions, which were regarded as a form of entertainment – all the better for being free – until their abolition in 1868. This particular song was about the notorious Sam Hall, who addresses the chattering spectators at the foot of the gallows – 'you bastards down below' – while waiting for the executioner to put the rope around his neck and open the trap-door from under his feet. An appropriate little number, this – given Hoxton's reputation as a citadel of crime.

It was a terrible neighbourhood that Peter grew-up in, with terrible people in it. But the majority, as always, were not so terrible – despite their poverty – which accounts for the popularity of another song, 'My Old Dutch' – a 'dutch' being Cockney slang for a wife, a duchess. It was a love song – all the more touching for being sung by an elderly husband to an elderly wife – and it was performed in music halls all over London, with a refrain that all of London must have known, including those at Westminster and in Buckingham Palace:

> We've been together, now, for forty years;
> and it don't seem a day too much!
> There ain't a lady living in this land,
> as I'd swap for my dear old dutch!

I should imagine that Peter would have enjoyed these songs immensely, because he was to become a very active Chairman of the Amateur Operatic Society after moving to Penarth in 1909. And that meant Gilbert and Sullivan – two other people whose songs were a comment on life in Victorian Britain, if a bit less gritty than the street-wise songs of Music Hall.

Various organisations – both secular and religious – were making it their business to help the poor of London's East End, including Hoxton, where the Hoxton Market Mission was probably the most practical. It ran a Band of Hope for young people who were prepared to pledge themselves never to touch 'the demon drink', or at least, never to touch it again. What could be more practical than that, when it meant saving money, not to mention lives? But the Market Mission also made a speciality of providing replacement boots for those whose footwear was reaching the end of its useful life, as well as for those who didn't have any in the first place. There were often queues of children outside the Mission, whether they needed boots or not. They might be waiting for some article of second-hand clothing, for something to eat, or for a chance to go inside and be warm for a change – unemployment or beer might have made it impossible to have a fire at home. Peter was never amongst these children, because he was never poor. But he would have seen them from his earliest days while he toddled around the market hand-in-hand with his older sister, Elsie.

When he was MP for Brecon and Radnor from 1929 to 1931, he volunteered for a parliamentary committee that dealt with the question of poorer children's footwear, which means that he must have rembered those sad little queues in Hoxton market for all of his life, especially as he was still asking questions in the House of Commons about footwear for poorer children when serving as MP for Newport from 1945 until his death in 1956.

But let's go back to the beginning again – or even earlier. The factory where Peter had been born was a family one, specialising in the manufacture of cigars – or 'segars,' as they were called at that time – the business having been founded by his grandfather, James Reykers Freeman, whose middle name had come from a Dutch forebear; like the 'h' in Bernhard, probably. In 1884, the factory and all that went with it was taken over by the industrious George – son of James and father of Peter – who began to expand it for all he was worth; ploughing his profits back into it, instead of spending at least a part of them on a house, which is why they lived in that flat above the workshops and the office.

Expansion on the manufacturing side was matched by an equal expansion in the sales force, which travelled the country by train, lugging with great difficulty the huge wooden chests that contained samples for tempting all those retailers – publicans, hoteliers, shopkeepers, etc – who were prepared to listen to their enticing little speeches. These commercial travellers – or reps, as we call them now – must have been delighted when Freemans went over to motor cars, thus sparing them the daily horrors of draughty railway platforms and halting conversations with fellow passengers.

In that flat above the factory, all nine children ate, slept and did their homework after a day at school. And what an amazing bunch they turned out to be, every single one of them! There were engineers amongst them, including Ralph, who designed the Sydney Harbour Bridge. There was Peter, or Bernhard William, whom *The Times* described as an 'energetic reformer'. (Very sportingly, when you consider that they opposed the actual reforms.) There was Dorothy – or Dolly – who exhibited her paintings at the Royal Academy; her twin sister, Daisy, who became the family doctor of Mr and Mrs George Bernard Shaw; while Elsie – another very good artist indeed – was to become the first Lady Sandford, wife of a Vice-Chamberlain at Buckingham Palace.

They all had social consciences, too – the most impressive in this respect being Arnold, who ran an Educational Settlement for the poor and unemployed in Sheffield for nearly the whole of his working life, and who used to collect for the Salvation Army on a Sunday afternoon, when they held their open-air meetings outside the gates of his college at Oxford, St. John's, where he got a first in History.

Arnold was the brother whom Peter liked best; he was the closest to him in both age and outlook, being two years older. They played together as boys, sometimes chasing each other over the roof of the factory – which Arnold described with relish to Grace Hoy, who had been his secretary at the Sheffield Settlement, and who passed it on to me with equal relish – plus a touch of admiration – over the phone from Chesterfield, where she now lives. This was the very first hint I came across of Peter's amazing physical courage – and Arnold's, too, of course – because games on roofs are not for the fearful, especially chasing games.

It was a happy life for all of them, despite the daily ritual they had to undergo before setting off for school, or going out to play, if it was holiday time. Every morning – so Peter's son, David, told me – they had to line up outside a room where there was a bath full of stone-cold water straight from the tap. One by one, they were expected to go in through the door to that room, immerse themselves from head to foot, and then go out by another door on the far side, where they would be handed a towel. But only if they were wet, presumably; otherwise, I suppose they'd be sent back. They were told that this regime would enable them to live much longer. And David was told the same by Peter when he, too, was expected to immerse himself daily in a bath of stone-cold water as a boy in Penarth. That's why I wasn't able to see him before ten-thirty in the morning on either of the occasions when I visited him at his home in Devon. It's a hot bath that he takes these days. A leisurely one, too, before sitting down to his breakfast and a paper. And, as he says, it hasn't shortened his life at all as far as he can tell, because he's already over eighty, apparently in the best of health, and looking forward to reading this book, whenever it might appear.

One close relative of Peter's whom I haven't yet mentioned is the most important of them all, his mother. She was the daughter of a Baptist minister, whose children were all brought up in the strict old way. And her name was Edith Marion. But I shall call her Mrs Freeman, because I've come to regard her as the mother of a newly-acquired friend, with whom first-name familiarity would not be appropriate. She was a remarkable mother, too, as you will see from the document I shall summarise now. It's called 'That Dreadful Year, 1894 to 1895,' and was written by Mrs Freeman herself, at the insistence of Arnold, for one of the family journals – in the original hand of the various authors and in ordinary exercise books – that he liked to produce from time to time, even after he'd left home.

The document shows where Peter got his physical courage from. And his moral courage, too. The year starts off well enough, with a family holiday at Herne Bay in the Summer of 1894.

'Bernie,' – that's our Peter – 'learnt to swim,' she says. 'And so did I, for there was an excellent though small swimming bath, and a good instructor. Bernie dropped out of the instructor's grasp while he was having a lesson and sank to the bottom. I was horrified, but the man took it quite calmly and said to a lady in the bath, "Just fetch me up that boy, will you," and no harm was done.'

A couple of the older boys – including Ralph, the future designer of Sydney Harbour Bridge – spent most of their time playing cards. 'For, at last, after burning and destroying many packs, I had given in… and I used to join in sometimes of an evening.'

That, I know, doesn't show any kind of courage whatsoever, either physical or moral; not for someone who'd been brought up to believe that playing cards was sinful. But I like her all the better for it; because it means that she was human, and occasionally weak. And anyway, she was their mother.

'We had a very happy Summer,' she says, 'all together.'

But then...

'We had only been back a few days when Arnold was taken ill... The doctor proclaimed it to be Scarlet Fever... and we secured a nurse to look after him...'

She was very lucky to be able to afford a nurse. Not many people in Hoxton could have managed that. But nevertheless...

'After I had bathed and fed the babies and put the other children to bed, I used to undress... put on fresh clothes which I kept there for use in the Sick Room... and... play Halma every evening with Arnold.' (Halma, according to my dictionary, is a board game of 256 squares in which the pieces have to jump one another.)

'When nurse returned,' – after her time off – 'I used to have a carbolic bath, even wash my hair, and then go to sleep with the babes or see after my usual duties...'

No sooner was Arnold better, than it was 'Dad's turn'.

'He stayed in bed, and I had to get a cheque signed on the Wednesday, and said, 'Won't you sign the wages cheque as well for Friday, and I can fill in the amount afterwards'. It was a good thing I did so, for by Friday he was too ill for anything. The Bank Manager... advised me to make the signed cheque out to myself for the whole amount of cash in the bank, and after I was able to sign cheques for the business all the while he was ill and indeed I continued to sign the cheques all his life.

'Well, we got in a nurse... and by the end of the week Doctor diagnosed Dad's illness as Typhoid. Nurse told me afterwards, she had lost her two previous patients and had made up her mind that if she lost this case, she would give up her profession...

'At last when the crisis came, his mind was completely gone with delirium. We tried to get a male nurse, as he had to be held down but Bernard came for a few nights to help.'

I don't know who that Bernard is, I'm afraid, but it might have been Mrs Freeman's brother, or Mr Freeman's. Or a cousin, perhaps.

'Then began a very difficult period of convalescence because Dad was so frightfully weak and obstinate... He began to get hungry and wanted solid food and was very angry because he was not allowed to have it. He called Don (Peter's oldest brother), and told him to give him a biscuit... and threatened to disinherit him if he refused...

'We hoped our troubles had come to an end, but it must have been about the end of March when Bernie developed measles... Well, one by one, the three younger boys all got measles, and also the twins, Daisy and Dolly... Ted (the next one down from Don, an electrical engineer) came home, but had only been in the house a day or so when he complained of feeling ill... bad news... Scarlet Fever again... Ralph did not seem well enough to go to school... Temperature 102... Diphtheria this time! He was very, very ill.'

She had engaged a nurse again, but...

'I used to get up every morning at five o'clock and wash everything in his room over with carbolic – including Sundays – for many weeks... By this time the Medical and Sanitary Officers of the District became suspicious... and thoroughly inspected the drains, premises etc... Nothing was wrong...'

Another trouble. Elsie (the oldest daughter) had been staying with Grandma; but developed a very sore throat, plus a temperature of 103.

'I took a cab,' – to Grandma's, that is – 'wrapped her up in a blanket and carried her downstairs … Grandpa and Grandma said I must have superhuman strength, as she was a big girl of 11 years.' Once she was home, 'she came out in a thick rash… Scarlet Fever again… I took night duty and nurse managed by day…

'Don and I were the only two out of the whole family who escaped during that dreadful year. We finally decided to leave Hoxton… and every morning when nurse came on duty, I went out house-hunting… I used to spend the days going about, get to bed at about 5 o'clock in the afternoon, and was up again at 10 o'clock to take on night duty.'

That, then, was Peter's remarkable mother, who not only saved the entire family during the whole of their 'Dreadful Year,' but carried responsibility for the business as well. And at the end of it all, she found the perfect new house for them at number 6, Woodberry Down, just across the road from the impressive entrance to Finsbury Park, and close to a tram route for both business and school. The property included a tennis court at the back, and a field in which they were 'obliged' to keep a flock of black sheep.

It was paradise. And it cost £600.

Chapter 3

The Very Colour of Her Hair

WHAT SORT OF SCHOOL, then, was at the end of that tram
ride from Woodberry Down? It was Haberdashers' Aske's,
a rather exclusive one, founded in 1690 by a provision in the will
of Robert Aske, 'Citizen of London and Liveryman of the
Haberdashers' Company' – which was transferred in 1898 from
Hoxton to Hampstead, along with the ten-year-old Peter. And if
the photograph I have in front of me is anything to go by, the
boys carried sacks over their shoulders, like the ones that old-
fashioned burglars carried in the *Dandy* and the *Beano*. Only instead
of loot or swag, they had books inside them, in varying stages of
neatness or scruffiness, according to their owner's disposition and
the ferocity of the teacher concerned.

Unlike some of the material which I've used for this biography,
the facts about Peter's academic career were easy to obtain. A
quick glance at the *Independent Schools' Year Book* in my local library,
and I was in touch with Mr Cheyney, the Honorary School
Archivist for Haberdashers' Aske's, who sent me everything on
record, including the photograph of those boys with the sacks.
He even sent it all to me again, when I wrote to say it was lost.
And then it turned up, as you might expect, once I'd received the
replacements.

I should imagine – having seen a good many of the letters he
wrote in later life, and even postcards to his family in Penarth

from trips abroad – that the books in the sack over young Peter's shoulder must have been reasonably neat, or legible at any rate. His school reports undoubtedly confirm this impression, but they also show that he could not possibly have been bullied for his many academic achievements, like winning the School Silver Medal for outstanding results in the London Matric, which would have entitled him to a very high place in the queue for entrance to that university – or any other – had he so desired. In addition to the purely academic reports, Mr Cheyney also sent me some photocopies of pages from the Haberdashers' school magazine, *The Skylark*, and it's what I read here which makes me so sure that Peter would have been left unmolested in the playground, in spite of being a 'swot'.

This, for example, is what it says in the Spring 1903 edition about his status in the Football First Eleven, when he was only fifteen (and Arnold, more than two years older, was captain): 'Freeman, B. W., plays half-back or centre forward, and is really a very smart player and a good shot; but is at present too lazy...'

This is the only time – in all the tens of thousands of words I've read about him in newspapers, books, Hansard reports, private correspondence and magazines; not to mention all the hours of conversation I've had with people who knew him well, some liking him, some not – that I've ever heard him described as 'lazy'. A 'busybody,' yes. A 'meddler,' yes. But 'lazy,' no. So I think I'll discount that opinion entirely – as the attempt of some junior master or senior pupil to sound clever at Peter's expense in the columns of *The Skylark*. Unless it was written by Arnold, of course – in which case, I'd have to say it was a brotherly joke. But assuming it wasn't Arnold, I can only conclude that the author of the piece

From Arnold Freeman's Black Books.

had failed to realise just how good a player Peter was – 'making the ball do the work,' as they used to say; instead of wasting energy by dashing around.

In the Spring 1904 edition of *The Skylark*, he is described as 'a clever little player'. And in 1905 as 'clever, capable, hard working and' – in succession to Arnold – 'a valuable captain'. I was glad to see the words 'hard working' in this last report. That's more like the Peter I've come to know.

The Autumn 1905 edition talks about his skill as a cricketer, calling him 'a good bat, a good field and a good captain'. It also says he was 'a long way ahead in the batting averages'. On one famous occasion, he scored 105 not out. Quite amazing for a schoolboy.

He never made his mark at the highest level, though, either as a footballer or as a cricketer, despite having the talent – for football at least, as remarked by the father of my school friend; the one who played in goal for Cardiff City (and also, incidentally, for Ireland). It was at tennis that Peter achieved his greatest success, after moving to Penarth. But the basics might have been acquired on that court at the back of Number 6, possibly in competition with Arnold.

In that same Spring edition of *The Skylark* – where his football is described as 'clever' – Peter is arguing in an article for the establishment of a School Debating Society, which could deal with 'matters of public interest' and which would also act as a training ground for 'the great orators and statesmen who might in due time be included amongst the ranks of Old Haberdashers'.

What confidence, eh? – writing those words at the age of 16. And for publication, too; not for some piece of homework that would be handed back to him in class – possibly without comment – and then forgotten. This is yet another indication of where he must have stood in the pecking order of the playground. And a year later in the Spring edition of 1906, there is a verbatim report in *The Skylark* of a speech he made at the Debating Society itself, now a going concern as a result of his suggestion. It argues for the adoption of a metric system 'in the British Empire', which was also – in those days – a going concern, though Peter himself was to have a hand in its demise, especially as regards India. He described the metric system as 'natural', since we have ten fingers; and 'important for foreign trade', since 'our customers in the metric countries do not understand quotations and specifications in British units'. He also points out – this youth of 17 – that in 1895 a Select Committee of the House of Commons recommended that 'the metric system of weights and measures be at once legalised for all purposes'; and after a lapse of two years be 'rendered compulsory'. Since then, he says, the metric system has been made 'permissive' rather than 'compulsory' – or, in plainer language, it was 'shelved'; until the early seventies, that is – Peter being more than half-a-century ahead of his time.

It's a very well argued case, exactly in the style of his later writings on what we would now call green issues and animal rights; though as he became older, he discontinued the practice of showing off his vocabulary by using phrases like 'our quarto, duodecimo, vicesimal system of reckoning', with which he spiced his argument for the metric system.

So, then: Peter was outstanding in his time at Haberdashers' Aske's, both as a scholar and as a sportsman, while finding time to establish a Debating Society. And as if all this wasn't enough, he also grew a moustache – or made a brave attempt – which was celebrated by Arnold in one of his 'Black Books,' as those hand-written family journals had come to be called. And here it is, that celebration:

> Peter, they say, is growing a moustache –
> Not the Apostle Peter, by the way.
> Another one with whom he must not clash –
> Peter the reprobate, as some folk say.

While copying out those lines, it occurred to me that if Peter really had changed his name in preparation for a role as Chief Apostle to Christ in his Second Coming, then he must have done so very early in life, when he was still in his teens; which, for some reason, I find unlikely. And the reference in these lines to the 'Apostle Peter' is such a jocular one that Arnold could not possibly have realised what his brother had in mind, or didn't take it seriously, which I also find unlikely, as the two were so close. And in any case, would a potential Chief Apostle have gone to the trouble of cultivating a moustache? That seems unlikely as well, since beards rather than moustaches appear to be the correct fashion accessory for Chief Apostles. No, he must have changed his name for some perfectly normal reason; such as simply not liking it.

Now for some more of Arnold's celebration:
Peter enumerates each single hair by day
And counts them over one by one at night...
'Bless thee,' says Peter, 'though thy growth be slow,
The time is nigh when thou shalt make a splash,
And very soon the universe shall know
That I am Peter of the Grand Moustache'.

What could the motivation have been for growing those whiskers, which he later shaved off? Was it because he felt himself to be immature – and therefore a little vulnerable – amongst the male workers at the tobacco factory in Hoxton, where he had begun to learn the business after leaving school in 1906? Or was it to impress the girls? It could have been either, but if it was the latter, then another interesting question arises. We know that he was to become a renowned Casanova in his maturity, but what was he like in those early days? Was he a prodigy, naturally gifted in the arts of enchanting women – a Mozart of seduction, you might say – or was he a late developer, coming to the great game of attracting a mate (or mates, as the case may be) after an apparently innocent young manhood, devoted to business, tennis and the growing of moustaches?

Arnold gives us the answer in another 'Black Book,' with an item entitled 'Cupid and the Freeman Family', where he takes each of his brothers and sisters in turn – from Don, the oldest, to Dolly, the youngest – and subjects their love life to a very searching enquiry.

'Romantic life' might be a better way of putting it for those ethically far-off times – not long after the death of Queen Victoria; but long before the contraceptive pill – when 'love-making' before marriage would in all probability have consisted in little more than kissing, possibly only flirting, and when paying court to more than one woman at a time – or accepting it from more than one man – would have been condemned as very close to adultery – amongst the stuffier sort, at any rate, and there were an awful lot of those.

This is what it says about Peter, when his turn comes up; though Arnold is writing in the first person, making it appear as if his brother was talking about himself:

> But for warm love, who could endure a world
>   so cold as this is?
> I love the fair sex, I confess. Here's to all pretty misses!
> Waists made to squeeze, hands made to press,
> And lips just made for kisses.
> Then here's to Joyce, Flo, Joan, Marie, To Susan,
>   Bertha, Bella,
> To Harriet and Dorothy, to Lillian, Lizzie, Stella.
> And sweetest of them all to me
> And dearest, too, my Ella!

He was a ladies' man from the start, all right. Or from puberty, which is much the same; though he had the sense – which many such men possess – to marry the one who was steadier than the rest. And more considerate. In short, the one with both the sweetest heart and the greatest practicality; while preserving the flighty ones for amusement only. It was Ella that he settled down with, just as Arnold seemed to predict. And I shall introduce her without delay – as she appears in the pages of the parish magazine for Highbury Quadrant, the Congregational Church that she attended, as did all the Freemans.

'My Dear Friends,' she says in a letter to the magazine dated May 16th, 1909, 'I have dreamed of a happy holiday at the seaside with some of my family at Britannia Row, who have never seen the sea.'

I had better explain that the 'family' referred to were children from the poorer areas nearby, who attended Britannia Row Mission, an offshoot of the church, where material aid was provided, as well as instruction in the rudiments of Christianity, including sobriety.

'My plan for this year,' she continues, 'is to count out six or eight of the palest, saddest-looking members of my family and go with them for a fortnight in August. Miss Freeman' – meaning Elsie, the future Lady Sandford – 'has promised to come with me, and between us we are going to make it the happiest holiday we have ever had… Well, perhaps I ought to have told you this right at the beginning. The fact of the matter is, I have already taken the cottage, because I knew you would help me… Will everyone who reads this, please send me a contribution, however small?'

She must have got away with it – as, of course, she deserved to – because on August 21st, 1909, she is writing again. And this time her letter has its own special heading, provided by the editor – 'Britannia Row Holiday At Seaford'.

'My Dear Friends, We returned home yesterday fresh and happy from our cottage by the sea. For seventeen days the sun shone and only hid himself for a bit to let a few rain drops through to clear the dust…

'We rose at 7.30, dressed and had a peep at the sea before 8.30 breakfast – spent all morning on the shore, where we had a tent to stow our stockings or to shelter from the sun – home for dinner and back again to the same spot, and then a walk through the fields after tea. Milk and biscuits at 7.15, after which we all gathered to sing our evening hymns… There was not even a headache amongst us, and as for the fever and disease so mournfully predicted for us – why! we're radiant with health and strength… I wish we were going tomorrow… it seems so dull and monotonous not to be cutting thirty two slices of bread at each meal.

'The one point for regret is that you seem to have been done out of something – you gave all the money and yet I had all the joy…'

She was wonderful with children and young people for all of her life. Quite a number of women have told me how good she was when they were Brownies or Guides under her… I was going to say 'command'; but it ought to be 'care,' I suppose. And when she became a grandmother, she learnt to do conjuring tricks for the children of her son, David, and her daughter, Joan; including the one of sticking a tiny picture to the tip of a finger on each of her hands, and making them disappear – fingers as well as pictures – by saying, 'Fly away, Peter! Fly away, Paul!' After a worrying little interval, they would be made to reappear again, with the words 'Come back, Peter! Come back, Paul!' The grandchild who told me about this was himself a Paul – now an Associate Dean for Research and a Science Professor in Wyoming – who loved the idea of his own name being used as part of a magical incantation, seemingly concocted by 'granny'.

Ella was the daughter of Sir Andrew Torrance, Liberal MP for Glasgow Central, Mayor of Islington and Chairman of London County Council. But more impressive still – believe you me! – was the fact that she merited a full-length satire all to herself in a 'Black Book,' one of the very few non-Freemans to be so honoured. Its title was 'Smudge,' presumably her nickname. It was written by Arnold himself in 1909. And it went as follows:

'Every person has been subjected to calumny and ridicule... One person alone remains with an unsullied and unmentioned name... The superhuman difficulty of the task made us delay...

'How can one paint the glories of the Northern Lights in blue-black ink? In utter despair we have at last decided to ask our readers to write an article for us. On the following pages we print replies to our request for opinions upon Miss Ella Torrance.

KIER HARDIE: 'See the inscription in the book I gave her. I could not help liking her if only for her fervent admiration of me.' (She had moved away from her father's Liberalism, it would seem, and towards the Labour Party; judging by the words that Arnold chose for Kier Hardie, who was then Chairman – which in those days meant leader – of the Parliamentary Party.)

DR. CLIFFORD (Doctor of Divinity, that is): 'When I saw her in my congregation for the first time... it horrified me to think that anyone should dare to be anything but a Socialist in the presence of that hair!'

TWINS (DAISY AND DOLLY): 'Ella is sweet and she's got lovely orange hair.'

A STILL SMALL VOICE: 'Would that there were more Ella Torrances in the world!'

What else is there to say, except that she would make the perfect wife for a Labour MP, down to the very colour of her hair?

Chapter 4

The Little Manikins

THEY WERE MARRIED at Highbury Quadrant, the Congregational Church where they had met. On the 13th February, 1914, six months before the outbreak of war. And they came to live in Penarth, a resort on the South Wales coast, where Peter had already been living for at least seven years; building up the family business in nearby Cardiff and making himself agreeable to the local women. Of course, he had been travelling back and fore to London during those years, paying court to Ella and talking business with his brother Donald at Head Office. He had also found time to be captain of the Old Haberdashers football team in one place, while making his way as a tennis player in the other. And not just any old player, either. But a champion.

Unfortunately, I've never seen a wedding photo, but Arnold's daughter-in-law, Peggy, has lent me some photographs of the couple during their first few weeks in Penarth. Ella is the very epitome of a new and obviously happy young wife. She's pretty, too, and fashionably dressed, with a skirt that reaches almost to her ankles and a nice warm coat, which must have been necessary as she's standing in a snow-covered field – about to throw a snowball at someone, presumably her newly-acquired husband, the photographer. The photograph of Peter – taken the same day – shows him sitting on a gate at the edge of a wood, a lithe and athletic 5ft 7ins. He's looking utterly relaxed, which is a quality that Arnold always envied in him.

'I mean to be like Peter for good temper and philosophic disposition,' he says in his private diary, which I read avidly despite the warning on an inside cover that to do so would be 'a first step towards the gallows'. That eulogy of his younger brother was written in October, 1914, the year of the wedding. A couple of months later, he describes Peter as 'imperturbable, rock-like, solid, cheerful, courteous – no matter what happens'. They were both good-tempered, it would seem, Ella as well as Peter; an impression that was confirmed for me by their son, David, who said he'd never heard them quarreling, 'in spite of everything'.

And what was Penarth like, their new hometown? Very pleasant, apparently, as it is today. And very exclusive, too, with an abundance of millionaires amongst its inhabitants; as many as thirty two, it was said. Most of these were ship owners who lived on Marine Parade, half way up a hill above the beach – pebbled, I'm afraid – with a view to Weston-super-Mare across the Bristol Channel. The town had a reputation for being a bit stuck-up, as you might imagine. Well, more than a bit. It didn't have a Fishing Club like anywhere else, but a Piscatorial Society. And the *Penarth Times* would often carry a report in its sports section about a 'Rugger Match'. Now, where else would they have used the word 'rugger' instead of 'rugby'? Apart, that is, from places like Twickenham, or Twickers. There was also the Penarth Tennis Club, which put a ban on membership for shopkeepers, whom they regarded as 'common'.

Peter and Ella lived at Number 3, Rectory Road – opposite that very tennis club which looked down its haughty, collective nose at various social undesirables, including the people they bought their groceries from. But not their cigars, many of which must have come from the factory in Cardiff that was managed by by their talented fellow member, B. W. Freeman; a name that appears on the Honours Board as Gentlemen's Champion for every year from 1911 to 1922, and then again in 1934, when he was 46.

It was – and still is – a beautiful house they shared together. Not as grand as the houses on Marine Parade, where the shipowners lived; but with a better view, as it was higher up the hill that rises from the Esplanade. On a clear day, they must have been able to see the Mendips in Somerset, if not the Quantocks farther west, or even Exmoor. Just how delightful it is – and how much they appreciated their good fortune – was brought home to me by a letter that Peter wrote to the *Penarth Times*. He was a compulsive writer of letters to the Press – which is lucky for a biographer – and this one is dated January 25th, 1925.

'Dear Sir,' it says, 'your reference to the white headed blackbird, which has been noticed in my garden recently, urges me to write and ask those who want to see him not to frighten him away by making too sudden an appearance at my garden gate… He has breakfast with us nearly every morning, together with some hundreds of other birds, and is now quite an old friend. Yours faithfully, Peter Freeman.'

The *Penarth Times* in those days had a columnist called Silurian – the name of a tribe that fought the Romans locally – who used to come up with some nice, whimsical stories, including this one from the edition of February 3rd,1927. Its heading is 'Excuse To Teacher For Boy Being Late – Had To Help Mother To Make The Jam'. And then it continues with, 'Nonsense!' said the teacher, 'How could you help to make the jam?' – this being long before the advent of the New Man; and even longer before the New Boy, whenever that might be.

'I did, though, Miss!' said the boy, very proudly. 'I fetched all the jam jars from the cemetery!'

Which goes to show that not everyone in Penarth was well-to-do. Some of them couldn't even afford to buy vases for the flowers they put on their loved-ones' graves, making do with jam jars instead. Otherwise, of course, those millionaires on Marine Parade would not have been able to hire servants, poor things! Or the Tea Rooms, waitresses. Or the docks, dockers. Nor would there have been a workhouse in the town, which there was. Or inmates in it, which there were.

These were the people who lived in an area which even the shopkeepers looked down on, away from the Esplanade, and away from the Tennis Club, too, though its most successful player was not ashamed to stand as their Labour candidate for the Urban District Council, stating in his Election Address that he was already experienced in local government. This was as a Poor Law Guardian in Hoxton – a Governor of its Workhouse – a claim that was to cause me a lot of trouble, and more than one trip to London, in an attempt to look it up in the Metropolitan Archives. At one point, I was convinced he'd been 'telling porkies,' as the assistant who was bringing me the documents put it. Eventually, I discovered that he hadn't attended any meetings – although he'd been elected to the Board of Guardians – because his father's death had meant a lot of extra work and a lot more time in Penarth.

But before he could enter politics – with or without a porky or two – he had to make his way in the business of cigar manufacturing, down the road in Grangetown, Cardiff.

The first of the Freemans to tell us about the factory was Arnold – in one of those 'Black Books' of his – and the account he gives of it makes very unusual reading, because the girls who worked there were all singing a hymn. And it wasn't the Grangetown factory, either; but a previous one in the city centre, just a few minutes walk from the old Arms Park, ancestral home of Welsh rugby. Actually, he hadn't intended to visit the factory at all, because he wasn't interested. He had come down from Oxford to witness the 'Great Revival' of religion that was sweeping across Wales from 1904 to 1905. He stayed with his father, who had bought a house in Penarth – not the one where Peter and Ella were later to live, but a more ordinary one – which was used as a base when he and Donald were taking it in turns to build up the business in Cardiff. It was to be another year or two before Peter joined them in this venture, as he was then still at school.

But meanwhile it's Arnold who is in Penarth; and what he has to say about his visit is by no means irrelevant to his younger brother, little as it concerns the manufacture of cigars.

'On Sunday morning I arose at 7.00 and soon left Penarth station,' he says. 'After a slow journey over a distance of twenty miles we arrived at Maerdy... and the snow was just beginning to fall as we entered a clean little chapel in the heart of the town... Everybody knew the hymns and often continued softly during the addresses and during the prayers... The Welsh tongue, the disciplined fervour, the magical transformation of colliers into apostles, the snow falling outside, all combined to make the scene utterly unlike this century of matter of fact and rush and science.'

He tells us that it carried on without interruption from about ten in the morning until midday, when Evan Roberts – the leader of this Great Revival – made his usual unobtrusive entrance.

'There he stood with his hair all ruffled, looking little like an inspired prophet. Indeed it would not have surprised me to see him lounging, cigarette in mouth, along the street... He spoke Welsh for about half an hour and then began asking people to stand up and say that they loved the Lord Jesus Christ... Several were converted and broke down, confessing their sins. At every conversion the congregation broke out into a glorious hymn of praise of God.'

And when it was at last over, 'We took our long, tedious journey home... I was glad to see Dad's face on Penarth station and gladder still to see a complicated tea, laid and prepared by Mrs Hodkinson' – who must have been his father's housekeeper in Penarth, also Donald's, and later, Peter's.

'On Monday I went over Freeman's Segar Factory at Cardiff... where the girls sang a Welsh hymn – the hymns are their national tunes – for my benefit. I ended by going down the whirligig fire-escape which will enable the building to be cleared of people in about three minutes.'

That piece of writing says a lot about the Wales that was shortly to become a home for Peter, and which was to remain so until the day he died. The Revival was still a fact of life when he started to commute between London and Penarth. And its influence can be felt to this day – some faint whispers of it – in the hymns that are sung whenever Wales are playing rugby, a combination of sport and religion which is very odd indeed, and even odder when you add beer to it in large quantities. But no more so than the combination that emerged in the 1920's and 1930's when Maerdy was to experience another sort of fervour, swapping Evan Roberts for Joseph Stalin, and Welsh fundamentalist Christianity for Russian fundamentalist communism, while acquiring the alternative name of 'Little Moscow' in the process. Or more likely, there was no question of swapping, because these two very different kinds of fervour – as different as the beer and the hymn singing – were to continue side by side, if not actually mixing. A double hope and a double reassurance in such very troubled times. This strange co-habitation of Marxism and evangelism – even within the same person, occasionally – was to spread throughout Wales, though in a milder form than at Maerdy, which suited Peter down to the ground, as he quite naturally combined within his own personality a deeply-felt if tolerant religion with a deeply-felt if democratic politics.

But let's get back to business. In 1909 or 1910, shortly after his father died, Peter became Managing Director of the factory where Arnold had been serenaded by a hymn from the girls. In *The Story of Cigar Making in Wales*, published by J. R. Freeman and Sons, it says that in 1912 Peter was 'walking along the bustling streets of Cardiff when he caught sight of a billboard advertising a Music Hall act calling itself 'The Little Manikins'. Quite who or what this act was has long been forgotten, but the name appealed to young Peter Freeman as an excellent one for 'a new small cigar', and this has since become 'one of the best known and longest established brands in the world'.

In 1914 – due to an increase in the demand for cigars – the factory was moved to those larger premises in Grangetown where 'the benevolent eye of Peter Freeman was a far-seeing one, and among his more important provisions were excellent social and welfare facilities. Indeed Freeman's were one of the pioneers of the Workers' Welfare Movement in Wales.' And in case these words are dismissed as mere commercial propaganda – coming, as they do, from a company publication – here is what it said about Peter's new factory in *The South Wales Evening Express* of October 25th, 1927: 'A fortnight's holiday is paid at Full Rate of Pay. Sickness Benefit is made up to three-fourths of average wages'. For all the workers, too – those on the bench as well as those in the office. Which was very unusual in 1927, within months of the General Strike, when the miners and just about everyone else had been defeated by the government and by their employers. But that wasn't all they did at the new Grangetown factory. Not by any means. The *Evening Express* went on to say that 'A Flat-Roof provides accommodation for roller skating'. And David Freeman, Peter's son, told me that his father bought a pair of roller skates – out of his own pocket – for everyone who wished to indulge in this bizarre if healthy occupation. Healthy if you didn't fall over the edge, that is. And as there are no reports of fatalities – or even serious injuries – I can only assume that the roof was surrounded by a wall; a fairly high one, too, and strong.

They were undoubtedly well-provided for, those employees at the Grangetown factory. You might almost say they were spoiled, an impression which is given further confirmation by a report in the *Penarth Times* of July 8th, 1926, about a 'Charabanc Outing', charabancs being the motor coaches of the day, but without any roof.

'Thirteen large charabancs, containing 400 0f the employees of Messrs Freemans Segar Factory purred out of Grangetown just before the breakfast hour, heading for the Wye Valley,' was how the report began. 'All the girls were gaily bedecked, and other workers hurrying to their employment stared in amazement at this huge cavalcade of singing girls.'

After stopping at various sights along the way – such as Tintern Abbey and Symonds Yat – lunch was served in the grounds of Abergavenny Castle. 'The party then adjourned to the river Usk; and as the sun blazed down on the crystal clear water, all were in a very Heaven of delight. Most of the girls discovered they could not swim; and of course the seven male members of the party had to show them the strokes.'

There was, apparently, a great deal of giggling, handling, and pretended swallowing of water; but 'the most remarkable feature of this swimming lesson was that the majority of the girls found they could swim perfectly – immediately afterwards – and went merrily up the stream on their own'.

A dance orchestra put in an appearance a little later, which meant that 'After tea, dancing on a hard tennis court was indulged in, to the great interest of the local lads. One eagle-eyed observer discovered that seven men were trying to dance with four hundred girls, and in less than ten minutes the whole male population of Abergavenny presented itself at the tennis court. To their great delight, they were allowed to come in; and the revelry continued until the homeward journey was commenced. Some of the lads followed the singing maidens on their motorcycles. That is, until a callous male member of the party broke their hearts by writing in bold letters upon a card the legend "FIRST STOP CARDIFF", and regretfully they turned and wended their way back to Abergavenny.'

Peter was an outstanding employer – in complete accord with his political outlook – but he wasn't perfect, I'm glad to say; as you will see from this next item, which was published in the *Penarth Times* last year (2001):

'On April 27, Newport reader Mike Bloxsome wrote to the editor appealing for information on the late Peter Freeman. In reply Gwynneth White, Chairwoman of Penarth Past Oral History Group sent us the following letter:

'I recall as a teenage housekeeper to my father in the late 1920's and early 1930's, opening the door to Mr Freeman more than once when he was canvassing in local council elections. He owned a cigar making factory, and his labour relations with his women employees were on one occasion distinctly strained over wages, despite his Socialist principles.

'My father was a railway auditor – covering much of South Wales – who often used the same train, which Mr Freeman would join at Grangetown station to travel home from work. On this particular evening, as my father's train stopped alongside the entry to the platform (at the top of a long flight of stairs from the subway underneath), suddenly through the aperture shot the breathless figure of Peter Freeman, a posse of irate female employees a few steps in the rear and baying for his blood. Quick as a flash, the ticket collector snapped shut the metal gate on the pursuing ladies, whereupon Mr Freeman swung round, removed his trilby hat and swept them a low bow, before diving into the compartment nearest him, whose door Daddy was helpfully holding open. Then the grinning guard stepped forward to close it; at the same time waving his green flag and blowing his whistle. And they were away!'

There's only one thing that bothers me about the contents of Miss White's letter – apart from apologising to her for leaving some of it out – and it's this: were those women really chasing Peter Freeman because of a dispute over wages? Or was it because of some adventure he'd had with one of their number – now sadly ended – which Miss White's father had decided would be far too delicate a matter for a widower to broach with his young and innocent daughter?

Until I started my research for this book, I had always thought of Peter on a bar stool; cigar in hand and a pint of best bitter in front of him, regaling his fellow regulars with spicy little tales about the goings-on at Westminster. It was quite a reasonable picture, based on the undeniable facts that he was an MP who had once owned a cigar factory. But reasonable as it was, it couldn't have been more wrong. He was a teetotaller for all of his life – and a non-smoker – who never went near a bar, unless it was to canvass for votes – which raises a very awkward question: how could he reconcile such a commendable way of life with making money from an addictive drug? Arnold was aware of this dilemma, as can be seen from a letter of his in the Highbury Quadrant Parish Magazine (December 23, 1910), where he says that 'drinking alcohol is bad enough, but smoking tobacco is worse'. Nevertheless, he did not hesitate to accept money from his mother for the various good causes he was associated with, especially the Settlement at Sheffield. The only explanation I can think of is that Arnold must have adopted the same attitude as the organisation he collected money for outside his college at Oxford, the Salvation Army, who would take money from the Devil himself, provided they could get it into the hands of God.

What could be more rational? Or more ethical? Which is my reason for believing that it was Peter's attitude as well, made easier in those days by a general ignorance of the dreadful long-term effects of tobacco, as could be seen by the number of doctors who smoked, even in their own consulting rooms. And in Peter's case, made easier still by a conscience that was less demanding than his brother's; if his (that is, Arnold's) private diaries are anything to go by, as I'm sure they are.

One way or another, the factory in Cardiff was to provide Peter with a sufficiently large income to embark on a political career, independently of any financial support from a trade union, which only a working class MP – like James Griffiths or Aneurin Bevan – could reasonably expect. And much of that income was to continue after he had resigned his Directorship of Freemans at the very early age of 41. Because as David – Peter's son – says, 'My father was pensioned off by his brother Donald at Head Office on becoming the Member for Brecon and Radnor in 1929. And he never needed to work again, unlike you or me.' This pension took the form of shares in the Company, as can be seen from the provisions in his will.

But for some time before his retirement from business and subsequent entry into Parliament, he had been serving a political apprenticeship in the affairs of little Penarth.

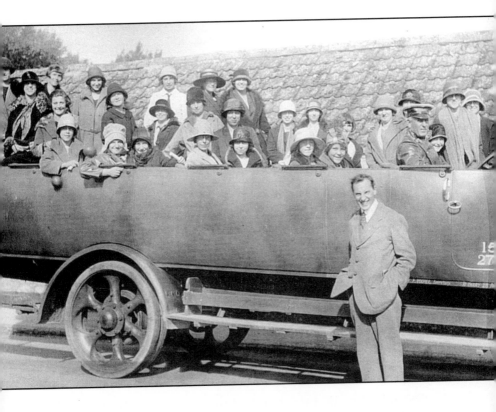

Peter in front of a charabanc of employees from the Cardiff factory on a works outing in the 1920s. Someone in the family – possibly Arnold – had written 'Put me among the girls' underneath – the refrain from a popular song which might well have been specifically written for Peter.

Chapter 5

The Fire King Affair

THE DAY I FIRST HEARD of the Fire King Affair was also the day when a lady came up to me in the reference department of Penarth Library – a lady in her seventies, I suppose – and whispered the words 'Excuse me, but I couldn't help overhearing...' She had seen the librarian bringing me a volume of the *Penarth Times* – bound in heavy-duty cardboard – and had heard the name of Peter Freeman being mentioned. So I invited her for coffee at the restaurant across the road; where we sat at a table on the pavement, with an umbrella to shield us from the sun.

'I was asked to a party in Mr Freeman's house one Christmas,' she said. 'Not by him, but by David, his son. My mother had bought me a new dress for it, too. And I think I looked nice. Or at least, a lot of people said so.'

She was still an attractive woman, dressed for summer. And vivacious, too.

'I must have been about sixteen or seventeen, maybe a little younger; and I thought that David was lovely. Is he still alive, do you know?'

'Yes,' I said.

'He married, of course?'

'Yes, and his wife is very charming'.

'Oh, I'm so glad! But what he must have thought about his

father, I don't know! Mr Freeman didn't make a pass at me. Not when he saw me with David. Fair play to him! But he made an approach to my friend'.

'Did she confide in you?' I asked.

'Of course.'

'Do you think you could tell me what happened?'

'I don't think I could,' she said. 'Because you'd put it in your book, wouldn't you?'

'Yes, I must admit I would,' I said.

So we shook hands and said 'Goodbye,' she to return home and I to find out what I could about Peter's political apprenticeship, culminating in the Fire King Affair; which was to be as good a test as any of how he had mastered his craft.

His first political act after moving to Wales – or, at any rate, the first reported one – is from the *Penarth Times* for December 21st, 1922, where he is named as a major donor to the Christmas Cheer Fund for the Penarth unemployed. It was typical of Peter to make such a donation. He was always making them. And it was equally typical of him to become involved in a public controversy, which he does a couple of weeks later on January 25th, 1923 when the *Penarth Times* published a letter from him, attacking the local slaughtermen for objecting to the use of a 'humane killer' that stuns the animal immediately. They wanted to go on using the old-fashioned pole-axe instead, which doesn't stun immediately. Or doesn't always, because much depends on the skill of the person wielding it, and his strength.

'Dear Sir,' he says in this letter, 'The obvious and simple way of getting over this difficulty is to cease the cause of such wholesale and colossal brutality as is brought about by eating the flesh of animals for food. But certainly, if this cannot be put into effect, the laws of justice and humanity demand that the sacrifice of these helpless victims of man's selfishness should be murdered in the least painful way possible. The 'humane killer', and the practical suggestions that accompany it, provide for this. The Council will be seriously lacking in their duty if its use is not insisted on.'

That was typical of him, too; because he first of all states the idealistic case, which he personally believes in, and practises – Vegetarianism – and then goes on to suggest an alternative answer if the ideal is not possible, which for most of mankind it isn't. In addition, he is taking a big political risk – something else again which is typical. Those slaughtermen at the abbatoir in Penarth would be amongst his most likely supporters when he stood as a Labour candidate for the Urban District Council. And they would have families they could influence. And neighbours next-door. And mates at the pub.

One of the hazards of research, especially on a hot summer's day, is the eye-catching headline that has nothing to do with the topic you are actually investigating. But which is useful as background – or so you like to tell yourself. There was the usual crop of these as I worked my way, page by page, towards knowing if Peter had made it onto the Council at his first attempt, in spite of coming out as a Vegetarian. Who could fail to be intrigued by the words 'Bogus Dead Man,' for example? – where a woman had been calling at houses in Penarth and district, asking for contributions towards the burial expenses of 'Mr Lewis', whoever he might be; a bereavement made all the more poignant by having 'only recently' buried two children. Except that there was no record of any Mr Lewis having expired in Penarth. Not within a year or two, or any children, either.

Items such as this were far more interesting than 'Labour Party Social And Dance At The Paget Rooms,' where 'Prizes were given by Mr Freeman'. And it's tempting to add that Peter would have found them more interesting, too. But he was a politician, seeking election, which meant the gathering of support from activists in his own party – those who were prepared to be insulted in his name on the doorsteps of voters they were canvassing, and who would even attend a Social And Dance for the cause, with or without prizes. A bogus widow would be nothing compared to this – however many children she possessed, bogus or otherwise – especially as there were girls in the Paget Rooms, longing to dance. With the candidate, if possible; who was still only 36, and by all accounts a charmer.

Well, he got on to Penarth Urban District Council as the result of a by-election on October 1st, 1924, becoming the first-ever Labour member to sit in that very exclusive assembly. And at his first attempt, too. But he'd only been there a matter of a month or so before he was writing to the *Penarth Times* again – on a topic far more dangerous for a politician than the 'humane killer'; more dangerous even than vegetarianism. He was espousing what is possibly the most unpopular cause of them all, the abolition of capital punishment. His letter, which appeared in the issue of December 11th, 1924, was about the trial in Hull of a man called Smith, found guilty of murdering his fiancee. And it went as follows:

'The Hull murder case calls for inquiry. One man kills his wife, believed by him to be unfaithful, and gets ten years (actually about seven if behaviour is good). Smith kills the woman he hopes to marry for the same reason, and is sentenced to be hanged. The Home Secretary should intervene if dire injustice is not to be done.'

There is a note from the editor after Peter's signature – 'As is known, however, the execution was carried out on Tuesday'.

It's a very powerful argument that Peter uses, unanswerable in my opinion – the anomalies of sentencing as between different kinds of victim, wives and fiancees – but all the logic in the world was of little account at a time when people flocked to any gaol where an execution was about to take place, waiting to see the notice of death being fixed to the gate immediately afterwards, together with any morsels of gossip about the condemned man's last hours that might filter out to them from inside the building. Newspapers published photographs of these crowds, with their air of quietly sinister joy as regards the drama that was unfolding only yards away from where they were standing, smoking their cigarettes and nudging each other excitedly at eight o'clock in the morning, a traditional time for executions in Britain.

The whole country would experience a similar frisson – if a more subdued one – as it made its way to work or to school. Yes, even children on their way to school, as I can distinctly recall, much to my discomfort.

Those who were horrified by it all were a minority, small and unpopular, who were often accused – as I'm told Peter was – of wanting to give aid and succour to monsters who prowled the streets, looking for someone to kill. It was impossible to argue back that terrible mistakes were made, as happened in the case of Timothy Evans – a tragic London Welshman – who was executed on the evidence of the man who had actually committed the murder himself, plus many others.

Capital punishment in Britain was finally abolished in 1965, which shows how far ahead of his time Peter Freeman was – yet again – with a letter that had been written in 1924.

A few months later (on May 21st, 1925), the *Penarth Times* mentions Ella – now a mother of two young children – who performed the opening ceremony for a Sale of Work in aid of the Labour Party; and was presented with a 'handsome' bouquet by 'little baby Griffiths'. On September 3rd, there's a letter complaining about the 'Carnival Queen Hoax', when the committee 'selected a man for the position'. And on November 26th, we are told about the death of Queen Alexandra, the Queen Mother, who always displayed 'the sweetness, gentleness and love of a pure womanly heart' up until the day of her passing to the 'Great Beyond'.

The next year, 1926, was the year of the General Strike, when for nine days the Miners' demand of 'Not a penny off the pay, not a minute on the day' was supported by workers in a number of other industries, including transport, who had been called out by the Trades Union Congress. It passed off very quietly in Penarth – according to the *Penarth Times* – except for a solitary lady 'who leaned over the railings of the Railway Station and informed those working that they were 'black legs'.

Peter gave the miners his unqualified and very public support in their dispute with the coal owners, even after the other workers had gone back to their jobs. And despite the fact that he must have been seeing a number of the owners at his tennis club, or their very close allies, the ship owners from Marine Parade, who were also losing money, since there was now no coal to be transported abroad.

It was at the time of the General Strike that Peter made his first entrance into politics at a national level, or the first that I've come across. It took the form of an open letter to the Prime Minister, Mr Stanley Baldwin, which was published in the *Penarth Times* on May 13th.

'Dear Prime Minister,' says Peter's letter, 'The unprecedented circumstances require some new method to secure an amicable settlement – some independent personage to call the parties concerned together. May I suggest that, subject to the approval of His Majesty the King, His Royal Highness the Prince of Wales should do this on his own authority?'

And now I have an excuse for telling you of my own – admittedly remote – connection with Stanley Baldwin. It came about when I visited Peter's nephew and his wife at their flat in London. These were Lord and Lady Sandford, the son and daughter-in-law of Peter's sister, Elsie, the one who had taken those deprived children for a holiday by the sea with Ella. The present Lady Sandford went through an entire family album with me, which contained photographs of all the Freemans as individuals; and as a group at the back of 6, Woodberry Down. There was also a photograph of a family friend, the former Prime-Minister, Stanley Baldwin.

I was invited to stay for lunch, where I sat next to His Lordship, who is confined to a wheelchair as the result of a very severe stroke; and communicates by means of pencil and paper, as he is unable to speak. But in order to make me feel at home, he had asked his wife – before I arrived – to mark an item in the *Radio Times* for that week, which was put in front of me as I took my place at table. It said that the 'Antiques Roadshow' was from Newport, the town where he knew I lived. I was also allowed to take the album home with me for making photocopies, in a Sainsbury's bag, and told to bring my wife with me for lunch when I returned it.

But anyway... 1927 – the year of that lovely outing from the factory to the Wye Valley and Abergavenny – was also the most important of all in Peter's career as a local councillor, because it was the year of the Fire King; an object which I'd better describe, or what follows won't make sense.

The first thing to say is that it was the Penarth town fire engine; as pretty a piece of Victorian engineering as you could wish for, driven by steam – at a comfortably sedate pace – and capable of carrying nine firemen, as well as the hoses and pump, though not the large 'Escape,' as it was called. This particular Escape – not to be confused with the small one – was the ladder for rescuing hapless residents caught in an upper storey of a tall building, when there was a fire raging below and spreading rapidly upwards. It was taken to such an emergency by four or five strong men, separately from the engine, on wheels that were six feet high, which gave it enormous momentum, making it capable of arriving at a fire long before the engine did. Its one disadvantage – apart, that is, from not fitting on the engine – was that it lacked a brake; so the men who dragged it along – strong as they were – could not possibly take it down a hill of more than moderate steepness, with which Penarth is plentifully supplied. And a lot of its tallest buildings are at the bottom of these hills, most inconveniently.

As regards the engine itself – the 'Fire King' – its boiler had to be kept permanently warm by means of a gas ring; and then, when the alarm was raised, it took about seven or eight minutes to get up enough steam – with plenty of wood and coal – before the vehicle could be coaxed into starting.

This was the situation when Peter became Chairman of the Fire Brigade Committee. Being the man he was, he resolved to do something drastic about it, if and when persuasion failed. And when something drastic did become necessary, what could be better than a false alarm at the Gibbs Home, where orphaned boys were cared for? What, incidentally, could be more fun for the boys? The only mistake that Peter made, as far as the latter were concerned, was to arrange the alarm at a sufficiently early hour of the morning for them to get to school on time.

From the Council's point of view, the matter was rather more complex. Peter's fellow members were not best pleased at being kept in the dark about this testing of the Fire King's efficiency, especially as the Press wasn't (kept in the dark, that is).

'Monday night's debate on the Fire Brigade has been described as animated,' said the *Penarth Times* (March 10, 1927). 'It would be more truthful to say that the time was occupied in pillorying Mr Peter Freeman, who stoutly maintained his position...' The report goes on to say that for about ten months he had tried to 'drill into the Council the falsity of their position with regard to the Fire Brigade ... while the Council were remaining placidly indifferent...

'The suggestion that the Captain of the Fire Brigade should have been informed was ridiculous,' said Mr Freeman, 'because he would not have been human had his brigade not been sitting on their engine, waiting to answer the expected alarm'.

The rumpus got as far as the *South Wales Evening Express*, which published a cartoon of the Gibbs Home alarm that amused a great many people; though not a certain Walter Hallett – of whom more later – Peter's enemy on the Urban District Council. From the *Express* it reached the papers in London, causing an anonymous letter to arrive at the *Penarth Times* from someone whose style of writing I think I recognise.

'Heigho!' says this correspondent, 'Here you are again, up and doing... Can you not see that your confounded proof of what might have happened will be termed a stunt... ? However, we hope from now on that every householder will kindly inform the Fire Brigade before allowing their house to catch fire...'

It must have given Peter a great feeling of brotherly support, that letter; which couldn't possibly have come from anyone except Arnold. Especially as it seems to be a personal letter made public. And it appeared in print immediately before the expected debate

South Wales Evening Express, March 8, 1927.

THE PRICE OF A NEW
FIRE ENGINE
LADIES AND GENTLEMEN
WOULD BE ONE
THREE HALFPENNY STAMP
PER RATEPAYER
PER HALF YEAR

AT A MEETING OF THE PENARTH COUNCIL LAST NIGHT
MR PETER FREEMAN (CHAIRMAN OF THE FIRE BRIGADE
COMMITTEE) MADE THE RATEPAYER FEEL EASY AS
TO THE COST OF A NEW ENGINE, ESCAPES, AND HOSE ETC.

with Councillor Hallett – that enemy I mentioned just now – who was firmly opposed to the purchase of a new appliance.

This debate about supplanting the old Fire King with some modern upstart – whose only merit was that it could arrive at a fire in time to put it out – was to continue in Committee.

It was such an important event in Peter's career that I decided to look at the actual Minutes, taken by the Committee Secretary. But that's all they were, 'Minutes' – or very brief summaries of decisions arrived at, with voting figures. There was no soul in them. So for the proper story – even if it was embellished a little – I went back to the *Penarth Times* (March 24th, 1927), which reported as follows:

'The air in the small ante-room was electric as Mr Peter Freeman (Chairman) took his seat at the head of the table with Captain Mayne, Chief of the Fire Brigade, on his right… and Mr Walter Hallett facing him. An awkward pause was broken by the Chairman, who calmly announced that the Council had referred the question of purchasing a new engine back to the Fire Brigade Committee, with power to invite tenders…'

Then there was a row – only a little one; but a row, nevertheless – which went like this:

MR HALLETT: The present Escape could easily be taken by hand to any part of the district…

CAPTAIN MAYNE: I beg to differ, sir!

MR HALLETT: And I beg to differ from you, sir! I think it is a wicked waste of money to spend £1,300 to £1,400 on our Fire Brigade… I do not agree to the old engine being scrapped. There is nothing wrong with it!

And now comes Peter's contribution – a clever one, like his football

– aimed at winning over the waverers. *Away from Mr Hallett.*

MR. FREEMAN: Even if our engine were at a fire, should another fire occur at the same time, we should be unable to cope with it, as we have no duplicate apparatus… We could retain the old engine as a standby…

A resolution in favour of inviting tenders for the purchase of a new petrol-driven appliance was put to the Committee, and was carried with only one member voting against, the implacable Mr Hallett.

But that's not the end of the story. What Peter had done at the Gibbs Home was undoubtedly illegal; and might well have resulted in a proscution, even gaol. Except for one thing – a secret insurance against the personal risk of losing his battle with Councillor Hallett, in the form of a letter which he now read out to an astonished committee. It was from the Chief Constable of Cardiff.

'Dear Councillor Freeman,' it said, 'I see in your local Press a report about the test call of fire… While I appreciate the fact that you did not mention my name as having suggested the course, I have not the slightest objection to the fact being made public…'

'Game, Set and Match to Mr Freeman,' as it might have been announced in his favourite sport. But such an overwhelming victory does not necessarily endear you to everyone, even amongst those on your side. He lost his seat at the election in April, 1927; and consequently was not invited to the ceremony at which the new appliance was accepted by the Council. At least, I couldn't see his name on the list of invited guests, hard as I looked. In other words, he no longer mattered; in spite of having been the cause of all those free drinks and tasty morsels.

But that's still not the end; because he was soon to find out how important luck can be for success in politics, as in life generally. On March 1st, 1928 – or St. David's Day, if you prefer – there was a headline in the *Penarth Times* about a 'Remarkable Explosion in Mr Peter Freeman's Dining Room'.

'Peacefully sleeping on Tuesday night,' said the report that followed, 'Mr and Mrs Freeman were awakened by a terrific crash, as of fifty guns... They thought that their end had come or the crack of doom was pending, but it was the anthracite stove exploding in their dining room, which awakened the whole of Rectory Road. Mr and Mrs Freeman went downstairs, where they found that the hall was full of a dense black smoke, which was coming from under the dining room door... Upon investigation, they found that part of the chimney and mantelpiece had gone... chairs and tables were ruined... It was thought (by an insurance assessor) that the reason for the explosion was a piece of explosive in the coal, a relic of some blasting at the mine'.

When interviewed about it the next day, Ella said she 'did not mind so much as no-one was injured'. Which was typical of her never failing decency.

But it's an ill wind... Or now for the luck, which I spoke of a moment ago.

On the very same page as this report – and directly underneath it – was an Election Notice, with photograph, stating that Peter was the Labour Candidate in the North Division of Penarth for a seat on Glamorganshire County Council, which a week later he is reported as winning.

And who did he beat? Why, none other that his oldest and bitterest adversary, Mr Walter Hallett. By a single vote.

The story of the explosion must surely have helped, mustn't it?

Chapter 6

Teetering on a Tightrope

THAT METAPHOR OF MINE about the tightrope, which I used in Chapter One – to describe the predicament of those who could neither give up religion entirely, nor embrace Darwinism wholeheartedly – doesn't seem so good to me now, on reflection. I thought it applied to Peter, amongst others; but when I bring to mind what Arnold said about his easy-going temperament – and how he envied him for it – I'm not so sure. Could it have been that what was a tightrope for some was a good solid plank for Peter? – enabling him to move easily between the earthly and the heavenly without any bother at all. No sweat, as they say.

And that raises another question: if he was so casual about this, could he not have been equally casual about about the Chief Apostle idea, which I thought I'd settled once and for all in Chapter Three? There might, for example, have been no significance whatsoever in his apparent failure to mention this to Arnold, apart from merely not wanting to. Or not wanting to see it reported – satirically, for sure – in one of the latter's 'Black Books'. And as for that beginner's moustache of his, it was probably as unconnected with any feelings of Destiny – with a capital 'D' – as was Hitler's moustache with his malice or Einstein's with his genius. What about my third objection, then? – the youthfulness of Peter when he changed his name from Bernhard William. Well, what about

Joan of Arc, who was only 19 when they burned her at the stake in Rouen, her mission complete? Or Jesus himself, who was a mere child when – according to St. Luke – he talked like a prophet to an astonished group of Elders in the Temple at Jerusalem?

It was to answer these questions – or try to – that I went every week for the best part of a year to a large old house in Cardiff, where the Welsh Theosophical Society has its headquarters, and where its archives are kept, including the Annual Reports that were written between 1921 and 1944 by its first General Secretary, Peter Freeman. On my first visit there, I was handed over to Ray Innocent, who took me to a library near the top of the house, where he'd put all the records I was likely to need on a table for me. He showed me how to work the heater, told me where he'd be if I had any queries, and left me to myself.

I had made it my business to find out what Theosophy was before I even made an appointment to visit the Lodge, as the house is properly called. And for someone who'd been brought up as a Catholic, it was utterly fascinating, because it was so different. Attractive as well, since it was undemanding, 'brotherhood' being the only belief that a prospective entrant must subscribe to, that belief extending to all living things, not just to people. Even more amazing, from a former Catholic's point of view, was finding out that you could, if you so desired, continue going to church after you had been admitted to the Society. Or to mosque, synagogue or temple; it didn't matter. This is why Peter was able to give the impression – if it was just an impression – that he thought of himself as as the right-hand man of Christ, despite the fact that he had become a Theosophist, and therefore a 'Hindu at heart'.

The society was founded in New York by an American army colonel and a Russian Countess in 1875, at a time when people of a liberal disposition were looking for spiritual guidance – in some cases, any kind of spiritual guidance – that would make Evolution more acceptable, or at least more palatable, than it was to those of a literal or fudamentalist turn of mind. And what made Theosophy particularly acceptable to such tolerant people was that it propounded a spiritual version of Evolution that had been accepted by Hindus for thousands of years before the birth of Christ, let alone Darwin.

This is Karma, which the *Shorter Oxford Dictionary* defines as 'the sum of a person's actions in one of his successive states of existence, regarded as determining his fate in the next'. It is, therefore, a form of evolution where you can go backwards as well as forwards; but Theosophists seem to believe that everyone – including Hitler and Stalin, presumably; also Jack the Ripper – will eventually end up in a state of bliss, or union with the cosmic principle, after successive reincarnations have purged them of all that is evil – which in the case of the above three gentlemen could well take millennia.

Unlike Darwinian evolution, which can bring about improvement only to the species, Karma will affect both the species and the individual alike, everyone, especially as help is given to us all by the 'Masters' or 'Mahatmas'; those Great Souls – Christ, Buddha and Mohammed among them – who appear on earth from time to time for the purpose of guiding us towards the ultimate goal of our 'Karmic Evolution'.

But I don't know why I'm struggling to tell you this, when it was explained at a public lecture in Newport – with Councillor

Peter Freeman of Penarth in the Chair – by no less a person than Annie Besant, the British feminist and social campaigner, who became World President of the Theosophical Society in 1907 after moving to Adyar, Madras, India, where its headquarters had been since 1878.

Here, then, is what the *South Wales Argus* says about her lecture, which was delivered at Newport Town Hall in October, 1925:

'Dr. Besant, now 78, wished to help those who believed in the coming of a Great World Teacher by giving them some reason outside of their faith… At the present time there was a sequence of events similar to those which had preceded the coming of other World Teachers… a great many earthquakes were taking place, and in the Pacific they would find islands which were the peaks of a new continent… She had another reason, too, founded on the unhappiness and hopelessness of the world. Things were in so bad a state that she felt the time had come when the cry of the miserable to Him to come and save them would be listened to.'

It was no wonder that Peter should have regarded the possibility of a Second Coming in such a casual way. Everyone else did. Or, at least, everyone else who was important to him.

Occult ideas of all kinds – not only messianic ones – were so general that characters who espouse them occur quite naturally in novels about the period, however sceptical the creators of those novels might themselves be. Anthony Powell, for example, with the sinister Mrs Erdleigh and her ouija board in *A Dance to the Music of Time*, and P. G. Wodehouse – as perceptive as any of them, but with better jokes – who has a 'world famous writer on Theosophy' in *A Girl on a Boat*. Or if we look at poetry, there was Madame Sosostris, a 'famous clairvoyante,' in *The Waste Land*, which was published in 1922, the same year as *A Girl on a Boat*.

Closer to home, there was the Penarth Public Library – just around the corner from Peter and Ella – where lectures on the occult and the mystical were constantly on offer; including one whose title was a question to be answered with a very emphatic 'Yes!' – 'Do We Believe in Angels'? This particular lecture was given by a Major Galloway, whose military rank could well provide a confirmation for my conjecture that an increase in awareness of things spiritual – and the yearning that brought it about – might have had as much to do with the hideous number of young men killed in the First World War, as with any reaction to Darwinism.

I don't know when exactly Peter became a Theosophist – he might not have known himself – but he was certainly a member within a few years of marrying, as was the ever supportive Ella; one of the volumes that Ray Innocent had put out for me was a Minute Book of the Penarth Lodge, where 'Mr Freeman' is listed as Chairman, and 'Mrs Freeman' as one of those present at the First Annual General Meeting, which was held in 1917.

At the Second AGM – in January, 1918, when the war was drawing to a close – Ella agreed to represent the Penarth Lodge on the local committee for the aid of discharged soldiers and sailors. And in February, 1919 – three months after the Armistice had been signed – one lady member, whose name I couldn't decipher, was offering to send a pamphlet entitled *Life After Death* to all 'bereaved relatives in Penarth'. Which is another confirmation of my surmise about a connection between an increased awareness of things spiritual – or supernatural or mystical, whatever you like to call them – and the four years of slaughter in France.

Peter himself gave a lecture at the Public Library in 1922 –

with a highly significant title, 'The Occult Side of Dancing,' combing two aspects of his complex, if easygoing nature. His agent when he was MP for Brecon and Radnor – Tudor Watkins, who later became a Lord – used to have quite a job getting Peter away from Labour Party Socials in the constituency 'whenever there was dancing and the girls were pretty'. I was told this by Tudor's widow, the friendly and helpful Lady Watkins. She also told me that her husband had great difficulty coping with the 'spartan' diet whenever he went to stay with Peter at Rectory Road. Sometimes he would have to 'sneak out' for more substantial fare, such as fish and chips (plus, no doubt, a couple of peppermints to hide the tell-tale smell on his breath. Or more likely, some deep breathing of sea air on the Esplanade, as he was a diabetic).

That spartan diet was always a source of amazement whenever Peter's energy was being discussed – whether on the tennis court or in bed – though not when his personal philosophy was under consideration, because a meagre as well as a vegetarian diet was an expression of the 'oneness' he felt, both with the animal kingdom and with his fellow human beings in parts of the world where famine was endemic. Arnold once wrote an 'Alphabet' about his family and friends – in the 'Black Book' of 1910 – and this is what he says when he comes to the letter 'P':

'P' is for Pear Pip and Piece of Parched Pea,
That for Peter is breakfast and dinner and tea.

That's what I meant when I said that the title of his lecture was 'significant,' combining the ethereal with the carnal. Less significant was the title of another lecture he gave, 'The World Idea'. But the content was about as significant as it could possibly have been, since Peter was giving an account of his attendance – in December, 1925 – at the Jubilee Convention of the Thosophical Society in Adyar, Madras, when he believed he had heard the voice of Christ.

This second lecture was reported fully in the *Penarth Times* ; and rather less fully by Peter himself in his Annual Report of the Theosophical Society in Wales for 1925 to 1926.

The newspaper starts off – with kindly exaggeration – by saying that 'Everyone has been looking forward to this talk by Councillor Freeman, who returned recently, tanned by the sun of India, to the fogs and rains of home. His references to Mr J. Krishnamurti, erroneously called the Messiah, instead of the Voice of God, will be of special interest…

'While in Madras, Councillor Freeman had lived as an Indian, wearing Indian costume, eating in the Indian manner, and even worshipping sometimes in a Hindu Temple…

'Adyar itself is a model garden village… with its own electricity supply, printing press and university. It is beautifully situated between the Adyar river and the Pacific ocean…

'There were about three thousand delegates from fifty different countries, Councillor Freeman attending as a duly elected representative of Wales… Practically all were vegetarian and teetotallers… drawn from every religion and walk of life…

'The daily routine began with Common Worship at six a. m., during which prayers were offered by duly consecrated officials from each of the Great World Faiths – Christian, Buddhist, Muslim etc. Temples and churches of each of these religions had also been erected; and following the Common Worship, the services of particular religions were solemnised in their own building…

'Words cannot describe the supreme peace and joy that characterised the Convention,' said Councillor Freeman. 'Brotherhood was demonstrated as a practical reality during the whole month of the Congress…'

'Mr Freeman concluded his address by stating further, 'I believe I heard the voice of Christ during my visit to India… On December 28th last… He used the voice of Mr J. Krishnamurti for this purpose when he spoke these words: 'I come to those who want Sympathy, who want Happiness, who are longing to be released. I come to reform, not to tear down. Not to destroy, but to build.'

'I believe,' said Mr Freeman, 'that Christ used the voice of this young disciple as a vehicle on this occasion, as he used that of Jesus at the previous Coming… He comes to proclaim the World Religion, whose fundamental teaching will be Brotherhood, and to prepare for an age of Happiness, such as the world has never known before…''

Three years later, Stalin had taken control of Russia; and the Labour Camps of Northern Siberia were beginning to fill up. Seven years later, Hitler was Chancellor of Germany; and the concentration camps were shortly to be under construction. Thirteen years later, the Second World War had broken out; and millions everywhere, happily enjoying their youth or their age, were destined to die an untimely death.

Which makes the questions we set out to answer seem irrelevant. Or trivial. But, yes – thinking it over again – I'm certain that Peter believed in a Second Coming; though it wasn't the Christ of Christianity, but a Christ who was one of Theosophy's 'Great Souls,' one of its 'Masters'. What other conclusion could I have possibly come to after reading the *Penarth Times* article, as well as

Peter's own account in his report to the Society in Wales for 1925 to 1926?

And now for that other, more uncomfortable question – the idea that he thought of himself as a latter day Chief Apostle, and had changed his name accordingly. Well, I can't find any evidence at all for that, I'm glad to say – because I wouldn't have found it congenial to be the biographer of someone who could entertain such ideas about himself. The Chief Apostle at Adyar was obviously Mr J. Krishnamurti, whom Peter recognises as such, calling him the 'Voice of God'.

Was he naive, then? Well, yes, of course he was. But as I've already tried to prove, it was a time when the supernatural, the mystical, and the occult were all taken seriously, even by those who didn't believe in them. At other times, completely different ideas – no less unsubstantial – have been taken seriously, even by those who didn't believe in them.

Take Utopianism, for example, which has appeared from time to time throughout the ages – most recently in the 1960's, and lasting for a couple of decades, roughly speaking. Its adherents were convinced that a workers' revolution was about to take place, led by young people (can you imagine it?), ushering in an age of Peace and Plenty – after a little judicious bloodshed.

No, I don't think that Peter's belief – for all its naivete – was any more foolish than that one, whose advocates seemed to forget that an ideal society would have to be lived in – and administered – by anything-but-ideal people.

If I have a quarrel with Peter, it's not because he went to Adyar, Madras, believing what he did, but because he stayed there so long, leaving Ella in Penarth caring for two young children –

Joan who was nine, and David who was seven. Even that wouldn't have been so bad if he'd gone straight to Adyar and straight back home again, but he didn't. Amongst the archives at the Lodge in Cardiff was a postcard for Joan and David from Paris, saying, 'Just off to Venice. Love to Mummy, big kiss to each. Daddy.' He was going to India by the scenic route, obviously. And there was another card – for Joan only – from Luxor in Egypt, saying 'A big kiss from Daddy', which he sent on his way back, following another scenic route. He also made detours to Palestine, Arabia, Switzerland, and Italy, where he saw Vesuvius 'in active eruption'. All this was part of his visit to Adyar. But at other times, he visited Copenhagen, Moscow, Geneva, Chicago, Vienna… I could almost say, 'You name it!' His visit to Moscow – and his observation of Communism there – convinced him of the necessity for using 'strictly constitutional methods in bringing about social reform, because the use of force will always lead to suffering and misery, especially for women and children'. And a visit to Vienna – just after the end of World War One – led to a number of 'little children' being brought from Austria to Nazareth House in Cardiff – the Catholic orphanage – as conditions in their own country were 'so severe'. A subsequent visit to Vienna will be dealt with later, when I describe the bitter-sweet consequences of a love affair in that most romantic of cities.

Arnold had been aware of these frequent absences from home; and had made a wry comment about them under a photograph of Ella. This isn't the slim and playful Ella who threw snowballs at the camera shortly after her wedding in 1914. She had put on a lot of weight over the years – had become matronly, in fact – and is no longer a mere captain of Guides, but a full-blown

Commisssioner, as can be seen by the uniform she's wearing. And this is what Arnold wrote:

> Mrs Freeman who sucks her thumb,
> Waiting for the husband who does not come!
> What's the good of waiting – get on with the work,
> So be a Guide Commissioner and do not shirk!

Quite a bitter little verse, isn't it? But this wasn't the first time that something of the sort had taken place in relations between the two brothers. A few years earlier, they had quarrelled over Theosophy itself – or its leader, rather – as you will see from this letter, which I photocopied, with David's permission, while going through his father's papers on one of my visits to his home in Devon. Though what it was doing there, when it was meant for Arnold in Sheffield, I don't know; unless it was a first draft, which it might well have been – since it was a painful letter to write, as the crossings out and alterations amply demonstrate.

'Dear Arnold,' it says, very curtly, 'Thanks for your letter and book. I return the latter herewith...'

The book in question was a scurrilous attack on Annie Besant, whom Peter invariably praises in his Annual Reports, calling her – amongst other extravagant things – 'our revered President'; and hoping that she would 'long guide the destiny of our Society'.

Which means, of course, that Arnold had made an unbrotherly mistake by sending Peter such a volume.

'What in the world must have made you change your opinion of Annie Besant is beyond my comprehension! – when I remember all you have said and done for her during many years, especially in the face of all the many social reform movements (which I believe you have at heart) that she has championed – Votes for Women, Vegetarianism, Labour Problems, Religious Freedom, Home Rule for India, and many others...'

Arnold was never a Theosophist – that is, a person who regarded Christ as merely one amongst many Great Souls. He was an Anthroposophist, who regarded Him as the very focal point of Evolution, entirely without compare. This is what I was told over the phone just now by Grace Hoy, whom I mentioned earlier on as Arnold's secretary at the Settlement in Sheffield. Nevertheless, he had long been an admirer of Annie Besant – before turning against her, much to his brother's fury.

'You pass on to me a book which is too grossly scandalous and inaccurate to be worth repudiating... If Annie Besant is the immoral imbecile which apparently you believe her to be, does it not strike you as strange that she should still be the head of numerous international organisations?

'I only hope... you will be as satisfied with your movement (Anthroposophy) as I am with mine (Theosophy). Yours, Peter'.

But don't forget that in between this angry letter (written in1922) and the bitter little verse (written in the 1930's, as far as I can tell), there was the letter of brotherly support which Arnold had sent to the *Penarth Times* at the height of the Fire King Affair. As nice an example as you could find of blood being thicker than water.

So it wasn't such a bad title after all which I chose for this chapter. Only, instead of bridging the gap between normality (whatever that might be) and Peter's relations with the supernatural, the tightrope I spoke of was bridging an equally perilous gap – the one between him and his relatives at home. Not forgetting the elderly relative – who was then a young one – who told Nicholas who told me about Peter's stupendous illusion, which has now been fully exorcised, leaving us free to deal with some further biographical mysteries, both public and personal.

From Arnold Freeman's Black Books.

Tudor's Motorcycle

O NE OF THE GREATEST obstacles that stood in the way of Peter's attempt at becomming the first-ever Labour MP for Brecon and Radnor was the *Brecon County Times*. In some ways it was a greater obstacle than Peter himself, who provided that paper with all the ammunition it could possibly need, free of charge. But the *County Times* was perfectly capable of manufacturing its own ammunition, even to the extent of enlisting the help of an influenza virus to extol the heroic virtues of Peter's Conservative opponent, Captain Walter D'Arcy Hall, MC, DSO, MP, an Old Etonian who was also the sitting member. And a local man, too.

'Captain D'Arcy Hall can stand a good deal in the way of exposure to bad weather,' declared the *County Times* in February,1929. 'But even his steel frame is not immune to the influenza germ. The 'flu has played him a dirty trick, spoiling one of those lightning campaign weeks with which he manages to keep in touch with his constituency.'

This kind of thing was happening so often – with scarcely a mention of Peter – that I decided to measure the amount of space that was devoted to the meetings at which they were adopted as official candidates for the 1929 election by their respective parties. Captain Hall was given more than 54 column inches, together with a splendid photograph. Peter was given less that 3 column inches; with no photograph at all, splendid or otherwise. But there was another paper for people to read, the *Brecon and Radnor Express*. When the *County Times* was sympathising with Captain Hall because of his indisposition, the *Express* – as, for brevity's sake, I shall call it – was carrying a report entitled 'Tramp's End – Found Dead On Hill'. He'd been there for weeks, apparently, and 'There was nothing on the body to identify it'.

Such a sad little item would have touched Peter's heart. And obviously, the *Express*, a mouthpiece of Liberalism – with a small 'l', too – would be much more kindly disposed towards him than the Tory *County Times*. It would even publish letters from him, something which its rival would never do. On April 11th, for example, Peter was telling its readers that the Labour Government of 1924 could not be blamed for the low wages of agricultural workers in 1929, especially as there had been a Conservative Government for the five or so years in between. The whole letter was very cleverly argued, except for one single sentence in which he talked about the earnings of agricultural workers in connection with 'other unskilled workers' wages'.

Every voter in Brecon and Radnor, the largest sheep farming constituency in the whole of Britain, must have noticed how Peter had included agricultural workers amongst the ranks of the 'unskilled' – including Captain Hall, who must have been delighted – and a very high percentage would have written in to complain. The one who had his letter published was a Mr David Lewis. And what a very good letter it was! 'To classify farm workers as unskilled is a common error for those totally unaquainted with farm work,' he says. 'And as Mr Lloyd George pointed out, it is absurd that a ticket puncher on a tram or train should receive a better wage than a skilled worker on a farm.'

Peter had put his foot in it, and no mistake. But there's worse to come, I'm afraid; much worse.

He issued a handbill, announcing a broadcast he was to make on the wireless from Cardiff, entitled 'Be Kind To Our Friends, The Animals', which elicited the obvious enquiry in a constituency like Brecon and Radnor, 'Does that include foxes?' And it wasn't only the farmers and their workers who asked this question. The miners of Ystradgynlais on the south-western edge of the constituency and of Brynmawr on the south-eastern – Peter's most active supporters – were none too keen on the foxes, either, which helped themselves to chickens from the sheds at the bottom of their gardens. And then, within weeks of the election, he described himself as a 'vegetarian' – in his Manifesto, would you believe! – an admission which the *County Times* was happy to comment on: 'Well, a large number of voters in Brecon and Radnor depend for their livelihood on the growing of meat,' it said, 'and they will not be in a hurry to support a man who holds views, which, logically followed up, would take away their living. Nor can we imagine the hardy colliers of Brynmawr and Ystradgynlais waxing enthusiastic for a man who would take away the principal item of their dinner'.

Now, Peter was a very courteous man; towards everyone, it would seem, including his opponent, D'Arcy Hall. So we can assume that his behaviour would have been immaculate when his agent took him for a meal to the home of a voter, as he frequently did. But all the courtesy in the world – and all the charm – could not have undone the disappointment that his hosts must have felt when he ate the vegetables only, refusing the meat; especially if the hosts were a mining family, who must have sacrificed a great deal to put a few good slices of beef or of lamb on the plate of their honoured guest.

When it came to Peter's Theosophy, the *County Times* decided that sarcasm would be a better weapon than polemical argument, saying that *Chambers' Twentieth Century Dictionary* had defined it as 'immediate divine illumination or inspiration, claimed to be possessed by especially gifted men, who also possess abnormal control of natural forces'. The writer of this particular article must have consulted a great many dictionaries before he found a definition as unfair as that one, concentrating as it does on some of the more outlandish aspects of Theosophy, which are optional. He went on to ask his readers if 'the orthodox ministers of religion amongst the following of Mr Freeman subscribe to this, or have they been spell-bound by 'abnormal control'?'

One thing that Peter had in his favour was a song that emerged from the playground of a school. I heard it quite by chance on a television programme to commorate a hundred years of the Labour Party in Wales, where it was sung by Eunice Stallard, who used to skip to it as a very young girl in 1929:

> Vote, vote, vote for Peter Freeman,
> When up comes D'Arcy at the door.
> If I had a lump of lead,
> I would hit him on the head.
> And there wouldn't be a D'Arcy any more.

Very good, isn't it? – allowing for the savagery. But it wouldn't have won any votes. Unfortunately for Peter.

The *County Times* would often carry a little item which gives another insight into the social traditions of Brecon and Radnor – apart from its hunting, that is, but equally unfavourable to Peter. On February 28th, for example, it reported on a Territorials' Ball, where 'The ballroom was artistically decorated with the regimental colours; and with the charming toilettes of the lady dancers and the mess dress of the officers, a picturesque scene was presented'.

Brecon was the garrison town of the South Wales Borderers, who prided themselves on having been awarded more Victoria Crosses for a single encounter – seven at Rorke's Drift – than any other regiment in the British Army. And both of Peter's electoral opponents – the Liberal as well as the Tory – had been captains in the pitiless battles of 1914 to 1918. There was another captain as well – from the Royal Flying Corps, predecessor of the RAF – who appeared before the election campaign had even started. This was a rival for the Labour nomination, Captain Wedgewood Benn, DSO, DFC, a future cabinet member. And father of Tony, the gentlemanly rebel.

Why, then, was Peter a mere 'Mr'? Surely he was capable of obtaining a commission in the army, with all his advantages in life – a public school education, social connections, money. And all the physical attributes, too, including courage, the most admired of them all. I began to wonder if he had been a conscientious objector; a speculation that was made all the more likely by the fact that he was Chairman of the Penarth Lodge of the Theosophical Society in 1917, a civilian at the height of the war. Peter's writings undoubtedly show him to be a person who was naturally inclined towards pacifism. In one of his many pamphlets – undated, I'm afraid; but absolutely typical – he says that 'The greatness of a nation consists not so much in numbers of people or the extent of its territory, as in the greatness and justice of its compassion'. And he goes on to write movingly about the terrible suffering of horses in the Boer War, mentioning a Memorial to them at Burstow in Surrey; which is dedicated to 'the mute fidelity of the 400,000 horses killed and wounded during the South African War, 1899 to 1902, in a cause of which they knew nothing'.

Can you imagine how Peter's advocacy of such ideas would affect his electoral chances in a garrison town? Especially when you consider what happened to Ramsay MacDonald, Chairman of the Parliamentary Labour Party, when he refused to vote in favour of War Credits on August 5th,1914. Well, first of all, he felt it necessary to resign his chairmanship of the Party, which in those days meant the leadership. His Golf Club in Scotland wouldn't even allow him the luxury of resignation. He was forced out. And there followed a torrent of vicious abuse in the press, including such an apparently urbane journal as *The Times*, which declared that 'No paid agent of Germany had served her better', while *John Bull*, an extremely popular magazine, was demanding that he be tried by Court Martial and shot — just like that! — regardless of the fact that Mr MacDonald was not a soldier. Some of the letters in those papers were even more irrational than the worst of these articles, but there were exceptions, including a surprising and very honourable one

WITH THE COMPLIMENTS
AND BEST WISHES
OF

PETER FREEMAN

from the Secretary of the National Union of Police and Prison Officers.

And Ramsay MacDonald, that pariah, was leader of the Labour Party once again, and leading it towards… well, towards a reign of terror, perhaps as dreadful as the one in eighteenth century France. The *County Times* must have thought so, because it published a cartoon of him as a Jacobin, a heartless revolutionary, with a guillotine in the background – ready for use on anyone he disapproved of – and the name of Peter Freeman as a prominent supporter.

But I still didn't know whether Peter had actually been a conscientious objector or not, which meant a trip to the Public Record Office at Kew in London, where I discovered that all the papers relating to conscientious objection had been destroyed in 1921 by government order – with a couple of exceptions, which didn't include Penarth, where Peter lived, or Cardiff, where he worked. So I went to a pub to think it over. The beer must have done me good, because it occurred to me before I'd emptied my glass that the Society of Friends was a pacifist organisation, and might have records of their own. I rang them up from the pub, there and then. They were absolutely charming, but they couldn't help me; nor could the Fellowship of Reconciliation, whom I wrote to later.

If I had gone to the National Library of Wales at Aberwystwyth before the Public Record Office at Kew – instead of the other way about – I would have found an answer immediately; not a complete one, but an answer of sorts, containing a surprise, because it was at Aberystwyth that I found the Election Manifesto for 1929, which – apart from telling the voters what Peter stood for –

also said that he'd been a private in the London Scottish Rifle Volunteers. Now, there was something to ponder on! Especially as I had recently been reading Arnold's diaries again, where he agonises on his own decision to register as a conscientious objector. And although he doesn't mention Peter by name, he gives the impression that their outlook on the war was much the same. But how could it be, if Peter was a soldier? And why was he a civilian again in 1917? Had he been wounded, or invalided out for something like epilepsy, which he might have attempted to hide, or what? And why was he only a private, with his money and his background, let alone his enormous courage?

Back I went to the Public Record Office on the other side of Britain to find out whatever I could about Peter's career in the army. But I was hindered again – this time by documents that had been damaged in an air-raid during World War Two, and which are known as the Burnt Collection. They had been transferred to microfilm, preserving the burns, scorches, rips and tears that had been caused by the initial explosion. I went through all the Freemans I could find – carefully, one ofter the other – without coming across a single Peter born in Hoxton, or any Bernhard William, either. But this was far from conclusive despite the amount of time I'd spent on it, because many of these documents had been destroyed completely. And some of the surviving ones were so badly damaged as to be unreadable in parts.

I decided I would have to tell my readers that I knew nothing about his service in the army, and couldn't even make a guess at it from bits and pieces of gossip, as there weren't any. This was, of course, a very unsatisfactory state of affairs, which remained so until it occurred to me that the London Scottish Rifle Volunteers might well have an Old Comrades Association, although they were only territorials and not regulars. It was their archivist, Mr Clem Webb, who told me that Peter had joined the regiment in 1908, aged 20, and they had lost touch with him a few months later – when he moved to Penarth, I expect. But he couldn't have served in World War One, I was told, or they would certainly have known. In that case, why had Peter joined the London Scottish Rifle Volunteers when he was so obviously a pacifist, both in his writings and in his general opinions? Well, we all do things that are out of character; every single one of us. And especially when we want to impress a future father-in-law – who in Peter's case was a Scotsman, born and bred in Ayrshire.

Peter was a pacifist who never had to prove himself – as Arnold did – by appearing in front of a tribunal for registration as a conscientious objector. And why should this have been? It was a long time before I could think of a plausible explanation, because I doubt very much if 'knowing someone' could have played any part at all; not when men like Gwilym Lloyd George, the Prime Minister's son, were at the front, risking their lives, and Winston Churchill, too, as a batallion commander after his resignation from the Cabinet, and just about everyone else, however good their connections might have been. You were either called up for the army; or you refused to be called up, risking prison if you failed to be registered as a conscientious objector. Or you… The first glimmer of a reason for Peter's exemption began to dawn on me when I was doing some background reading about the First World War; which included a reference to the Rev. Studdert Kennedy – otherwise known as Woodbine Wille – the Church of England clergyman who went about the trenches, encouraging the men and listening to their fears. But he also gave them Woodbine cigarettes – hence the nickname – which were paid for out of charitable donations.

Peter was a tobacco manufacturer at a time when a cigarette was essential for the fighting man, or possibly a cigar, if he was an officer. Enduring a bombardment while craving for a smoke doesn't bear thinking about – as the generals must have known, however remote they were from any actual danger; likewise the bureaucrats in far distant Whitehall, who were responsible for interpreting the regulations, which included any exemptions. Fine; but such an explanatiion raises another question again, just as awkward. Why on earth did Peter mention that youthful indiscretion with the London Scottish Rifle Volunteers in his Election Manifesto at Brecon and Radnor? Could anything have been more foolish, with all those captains about, not to mention the decorations they had been awarded for their bravery. In Penarth, when putting up for the Council, he had claimed to be a Poor Law Guardian at Hoxton, neglecting to mention that he had never attended a meeting, and he had got away with it. Perhaps he was hoping for the same casual treatment at Brecon and Radnor. If so, he was in for a shock. But not from Captain Wedgewood Benn – his rival for the Labour nomination – who had already been defeated by our Peter. Not from Captain Cemlyn Jones, the Liberal, who was more concerned about farming, being a farmer himself. And not from Captain Hall, who didn't need to; because the *County Times* was more than pleased to act on his behalf. And the following is a typical example, taken from the very same article that had dealt so briskly with Peter's vegetarianism and his Theosophy:

'Mr Freeman's merits, as advertised in his election manifesto, include "Private, London Scottish Rifle Volunteers". What is this meant to suggest? Are we far wrong in saying that evidently the hope is that some at least of the Brecon and Radnor electors will take it as meaning that the well-to-do Socialist served his country during the war?'

They asked the question over and over again. 'Were you in the fighting, Mr Freeman? Or weren't you? We demand to know.'

And yet, somehow or other, he managed to win, despite the long saga of mistake and misfortune that I've so far related in this chapter. What, then, did he have in his favour? Let's deal with the political reasons immediately, going on later to the much more interesting personal ones. Firstly, there was an electoral trend, covering the whole of Britain, that brought Labour up from 151 seats in 1924 to 287 seats in 1929. Another electoral trend – also covering the whole of Britain – meant that a Liberal vote in a three-cornered contest would be of greater benefit to Labour than to the Conservatives. In Brecon and Radnor, Captain D'Arcy Hall and Captain Cemlyn Jones were neck and neck, being separated by only 145 votes; which allowed Peter to slip in ahead of them both, like the cunning player of games that he'd always been. And, lastly, there were those miners of Ystradgynlais and Brynmawr and their wives who were solidly Labour, regardless of the dietary peculiarities of any particular candidate.

Amongst the minutes of the Executive Committee of the Brecon and Radnor Labour Party for January, 1927 is this little item – 'Cost of fighting an election estimated as £650 to £900, whereas the total of our funds at present is £5'. Now that may sound like another tale of woe, but not when followed by another item – almost as small – taken from the minutes for the meeting of May, 1927: 'Seeing that Mr Freeman of Penarth is the best proposition we have got, or are likely to get, we decided to recommend him for adoption as our prospective candidate, subject to the money difficulty being overcome'. In other words, Peter was adopted, rather grudgingly it would seem, because he was not just a Socialist, but a wealthy one, as the *County Times* had said in another, less happy connection. His rival for adoption, Captain Wedgewood Benn – although not short of a bob or two himself – had already dropped out, presumably because Peter had hinted at a greater readiness to dip his hand in his pocket. And such mercenary considerations were essential in a constituency that was believed to be 'unwinnable' – and therefore unlikely to attract any funding from a trade union, whether mining or agricultural.

We are dealing with personal matters now, of course, not purely political ones, and another benefit that Peter's money brought was the full-time help of Tudor Watkins, who became the Organising Secretary and Election Agent for the whole constituency. His application form for the post – at a salary of £10 per month, including expenses – could well be described as a thing of beauty, so perfectly is it typed, filling every bit of available space. It lists his qualifications as practical experience in both mining and agriculture; being bilingual in English and Welsh; proficiency in shorthand; and lastly, under the heading of 'Any Other Useful Remarks', the ownership of a motorcycle. This was every bit as important as political guile – or even literacy itself – in a constituency the size of Brecon and Radnor, covering an area of more than 2,000 square miles. One quality that Tudor failed to mention was 'diplomacy,' though he possessed it in abundance, which was just as well with a candidate who described farm work as 'unskilled' and himself as a 'vegetarian'. Just about the only statement from the Election Manifesto that Tudor never had to explain away was Peter's claim to have been one of a doubles partnership which had defeated the reigning Wimbledon champions.

As a candidate for parliament, Peter was a mere novice, but when it came to women, he certainly wasn't; anything but. And on May 9th,1929, the *Brecon and Radnor Express* had carried an editorial entitled 'The Woman Voter' in which it said that 'Voting Lists show a preponderance of women… and what women want today is the abolition of war'. Could it have been that D'Arcy Hall's rank and decorations were a hindrance with the woman voter? And that Peter's very lack of them wasn't? Even an advantage, perhaps?

If it were any other candidate, I would leave the question open. But it wasn't any other candidate, not in Brecon and Radnor; it was Peter Freeman, a born-again Pacifist. And a ladies' man, too.

He won by a handful of votes – 187 to be exact – but a Victory Celebration was nevertheless held, and quite rightly, too, at the Church Hall in Builth Wells. 'Musical selections were provided during tea through the medium of a gramophone,' said the *Express* in its report of this orgy. 'And later in the evening a Ball was held, music being supplied by the Cambrian Dance Band, lasting from 9.00 p.m. to 1.00 a.m.' This may well have been the first of those occasions when Tudor Watkins had to exercise another kind of skill on behalf of his candidate, a very ticklish one; that of extricating him from a late-night dance, when the girls were pretty and Ella was at home in Penarth.

Chapter 8

A Nice Display for Mr Speaker

I T'S MORE THAN an hour's drive from Builth Wells to Penarth. And no doubt Peter would have got into bed at once, longing to close his eyes. But Ella must have wanted to hear about the celebration first; every single detail, whether embarrassing or not. What was the food like? And the speeches? And the Band? And did he have a dance with anyone special, and if so… ? But eventually he would have fallen asleep, utterly worn out. Unlike his party leader, Ramsay MacDonald, who must have been thinking about the government he would form; whether in bed or not and whether alone or not. This was a tricky problem – enough to give anyone insomnia – because the Labour Party had failed to obtain an overall majority in the Commons, making it dependent on the votes of the 59 Liberal MP's. And all of these 59 would have had very strong views on some of the people that Mr MacDonald might otherwise have chosen as Ministers.

The *County Times*, like many another paper, set about the joyful task of bringing this government down – in its present embryonic form, if possible – by playing on the fears of those 59 suspicious Liberals. In a major editorial, it craftily reminded its readers of what it chose to call 'Labour's Golden Era', when it had 'provided a refuge' for left-wing dissenters of all kinds, including – a nice touch, this – 'nut eaters and sandal wearers'. But no longer, it would seem, because the *County Times* went on to say, with many an expression of regret, that 'the intending recruit to Labour does not find himself on the threshold of a political Arcadia any more; he finds himself in the guardroom of a Prussian regiment'. In other words, now that Labour was in power, the ordinary members of parliament would have to do as they was told. Or else... The staff at the *County Times* knew perfectly well that the Liberal Party was also not averse to nut eaters, or even sandal wearers. In moderation, of course. But with its individualistic and pacifist tendencies, it would certainly not support a government that resembled the guardroom of a Prussian regiment, where the inmates were given a diet of bread and water, supplemented by the occasional flogging. And Peter would have found it even less congenial than the average Liberal – being a nut eater himself, if not a sandal wearer – so we'd better enquire about his behaviour under this new regime, and the punishments he was subjected to.

That 'Prussian' editorial was in August, 1929. But scarcely three months later, the *County Times* was in a somewhat different mood, with an editorial expressing outrage that as many as thirty Labour MP's were criticising their leaders for not yet paying a pound a week to every unemployed man, as had been promised during the election. A pound a week is unrealisic, it said. Money doesn't grow on trees, or even on the backs of sheep. And amongst those thirty rebels was the member for Brecon and Radnor. On 12th December, there's a report about Peter's opposition to corporal punishment in schools which he expressed in the House of Commons, much to the amusement of a great many honourable members – both government and opposition. And a week later, he was asking the Home Secretary 'whether, in view of the cruelty involved by hunting, he would arrange for a public enquiry into all forms of sport in which the suffering of animals was involved?'

Peter was not ecactly cowed by this new regime, as you can see. He was making a nuisance of himself from the very start of his parliamentary career, regardless of what the party leaders might have thought. And he went on making a nuisance of himself, whether they liked it or not. While they, in their turn, were not behaving like the military policemen in a Prussian guard room – or a British one, if it comes to that. Peter was never flogged or put on bread and water, as far as I can tell; nor did he face suspension from the parliamentary party. In fact, he didn't even have to put up with any sarcasm from the ministers he questioned, who treated him with the utmost courtesy.

The *County Times* was wrong, then, quite obviously. But it wasn't going to admit it. Not as long as it could perform a conjuring trick with people's fears.

'The official government policy is to be as reasonable as possible in the hope that the electors may send the party back with an overall majority,' it said. And then it went on to issue a dire warning about what might happen if this were the case, and Labour was no longer in need of those 59 Liberal votes. 'The difference between the mild men on the Front Bench and the wild men on the Back Benches is one of tactics pure and simple'.

That was printed in March, 1930, the year when the peasants of Russia were being deprived of their land in the drive towards collectivization, and machine gunned if they complained too vigorously. The *County Times* was implying – none too subtly – that this could be the fate of tenant farmers in Brecon and Radnor, should the Labour Party ever be in absolute control. But meanwhile, those same tenant farmers went on protesting for all they were worth – about all sorts of things – not caring if their names were being noted in some Big Black Book at Labour Party Headquarters in London. Take Luther Howells, for example, who wrote as follows to the Breconshire Education Committee, which was itself under Labour control:

'Gentlemen – My child on the morning of May 31st, 1929, went to school with his Liberal badge on his little jacket, and the schoolmaster made him take it off. His mother, being annoyed, sewed it on for the afternoon session, and the same thing happened again, but at the same time there were two children in the class with Labour badges on, who were not asked to take them off. What I want to know, Gentlemen, is: are we going to allow this sort of thing to go on? If this is going to continue, the atmosphere of the school will be like that of Moscow. Yours etc'.

This was first reported in the Liberal *Express*, which treated the matter with great good humour, pointing out that Mr Howells had decided to take no further action; after a diplomatic mission – headed by the Director of Education himself, the servant of a Labour authority – had gone to the trouble of visiting Mr Howells at his farm. A week later, this same letter was reproduced in the *County Times*, which put a totally different slant on it – or spin, if you prefer – by stating that 'The Labour Party is notorious for intolerence and persecution'.

About the only thing that Peter Freeman and Adolf Hitler had in common was that they both expressed a concern for the welfare of lobsters; and in particular for the way in which they were cooked, while still alive. So it was an odd coincidence that Peter should have raised the matter as a parliamentary question in 1930, the year when Hitler led the Nazis to their first electoral triumph, the winning of more than a 100 seats in the Reichstag – a big step along the road to abolishing democracy in Germany. It's just as well that the *County Times* knew nothing of Hitler's one humanitarian instinct; otherwise they might have published a cartoon of Peter as his double, with a fussy moustache and a swastika armband. It would have made a nice little addition to their report of his parliamentary question about the cooking of lobsters for the House of Commons dining room, which went as follows:

'Mr Freeman asked Mr Compton, Chairman of the Kitchen Committee, 'whether, in view of the fact that groans and cries can be heard for a considerable time after the lobster is immersed in boiling water, will he not prohibit it from the House?'

Commander Southby (Conservative, Epsom) interrupted to ask, 'Will he also take steps to prevent the brutal method of eating live oysters?' (Laughter).

Mr Compton replied, 'I deny the suggestion that there is anything in the nature of cries from the fish. If Mr Freeman will provide a humane killer for the lobsters, I shall be pleased to have it used'. (Renewed Laughter).

For the rest of his term as MP for Brecon and Radnor, the *County Times* would refer to Peter – when it was in jocular mood – as 'the friend of boiled lobsters'. Or, more comprehensively, as 'the friend of boiled lobsters and naughty children'. The editorial staff must have been furious that they couldn't finish him off – once and for all – over the affair of the pretty flowers. But they couldn't. In fact, they didn't even report it, leaving this to the broader-minded *Express*. Under the perfectly bland heading of 'Mr Freeman's Suggestion,' it told its readers in May, 1930 – and without a single facetious comment – that he was to ask Mr

Lansbury, the Commissioner For Works, if he would provide a supply of flowers in the rooms at the House of Commons, stating that his only object was 'to bring a little more dignity and beauty to the place'. He could see no reason why there shouldn't also be a nice display – in an attractive vase – on the table in front of Mr Speaker. And added that 'The flowers would cost nothing, as there are plenty to spare in the Royal Parks, which are under Mr Lansbury's jurisdiction'.

So why did the *County Times* give this flower question a miss, when it might have allowed them a good, long sneer at Peter's expense? It could have escaped their notice, of course; when the report came in from their agency in London. Or when their political correspondent was going through Hansard. But I don't think so. It's much more likely that they were totally bemused by

From Arnold Freeman's Black Books.

A VEGETARIAN REPAST IN MR. PETER FREEMAN'S OFFICE

it; since Peter's reputation as a womaniser made it impossible for them to employ the obvious innuendo about a man who loved flowers – obvious in that homophobic age, I mean. And they couldn't think of another angle that was equally damning.

Peter was certainly busy, then. And not only with issues that were close to his heart, such as animal rights. He was also a good 'constituency' MP, which even the *County Times* could never deny. In July, 1930, it reported him as asking the Minister of Agriculture 'whether he can state how many applications have been received for permission to pay less than the prescribed rate under the Agricultural Wages (Regulation) Act, how many have been granted, and the extent of the remission, if any, in Breconshire and Radnorshire during the last twelve months?' It would be easy to say that Peter was trying to make up for his gaffe about farm work being 'unskilled', but it would also be wrong. His concern for the poorest among his constituents was absolutely genuine – there is no doubt of that – since he went on campaigning for them with the utmost persistence. And not only the poorest; all of them. In June, 1930, the *Express* carried a report of his question to the Postmaster General about 'the minimum conditions necessary to establish a telephone exchange and telephone call office' in the remoter parts of Britain. Because of course, there were no such things as mobile phones, and older people in rural areas like Brecon and Radnor were becoming increasingly isolated as their children and grandchildren moved to the cities – as far away as Birmingham, very often – in search of better opportunities. All in all, he was 'one of the most active members of the House of Commons,' according to a report that was sent to the *Express* by Tudor Watkins in 1931. And possibly to the *County Times* as well; though it was only the *Express* which printed it. 'Mr Freeman,' said this report, 'is a member of Grand Committee A, dealing with the Agricultural Bill, Land Drainage Bill, the Humane Slaughter of Animals Bill, the Rights of Workmen's Compensation Bill, the Children (Provision of Footwear) Bill and the Sentence of Death (Expectant Mothers) Bill. He is also Chairman of the Labour Group on India'.

The last but one of those items on Tudor's list is so terrible to think of – and therefore so compelling – that it ought to be dealt with more fully, and straightaway. An expectant mother who had been sentenced to death was often the victim of an extremely violent husband, and was defending her unborn child as much as herself. It was for this reason, amongst others, that the execution of pregnant women had already been abolished, the last one having been carried out in the middle of the previous century. Nevertheless, an expectant mother was still required to listen while the judge pronounced sentence of death upon her – 'that you be taken away to a place of execution and hanged by the neck until dead' – no matter how extenuating the circumstances might have been. Then the woman would have to wait for her official reprieve, which came from the monarch via the Home Secretary. It was a pointless as well as a barbaric ritual, which must have had appalling effects upon a woman about to give birth, and on the child in her womb. One judge so disliked this duty that he would beg the woman in the dock not to listen; and mumbled so indistinctly that even the Clerk of the Court was unable to hear what he said. According, that is, to a Hansard report on the Bill, whose purpose was to avoid such unnecessary pain by doing away with the ritual.

On that same day, there was an item in the *Express* that gave the results of an egg-laying competition for farmers' wives (or more correctly, for the hens they kept), and another that went as follows:

'In pursuance of his vegetarian zeal, Mr Peter Freeman is organising a dinner amongst vegetarian members of the Commons and the Lords; and the catering authorities are ready to respond with a selection of dishes which will do justice to the cult. The member for Brecon and Radnor has secured one notable acceptance, that of the young Marquis of Clydesdale, who has been so famous in the boxing ring. Amongst the Conservative vegetarians are Lt. Colonel Moore and Sir Robert Gower, and the Socialist guests will include Mr George Lansbury'.

Coming across a story like that – and quite unexpectedly – is one of the joys of research. Imagine it! A marquis who was also a boxer and a vegetarian. Who would have thought it possible, if they had come across it in the pages of Agatha Christie? And it looked as if Peter had been forgiven for his speech about the boiling of lobsters alive. By the kitchen staff, at any rate.

On November 20th, 1930, the *County Times* was telling its readers about 'Mr Freeman's Latest, The Elephants And The Asses,' a headline that would surely have whetted the apetite of Peter's enemies. 'Whenever there is a rum question on the Commons Order Paper, the author can be guessed at once,' said the report. 'So nobody was surprised when Mr Freeman sought to discover if the Home Secretary proposes to prohibit elephants in public processions. "I have no power to do so", Mr Clynes assured him kindly.

"Then will he prohibit asses?" put in Mr Kirkwood, and the Commons took the point appreciatively.'

The report made it clear that Mr Kirkwood's interjection had triggered off a great deal of laughter throughout the entire Chamber, made all the more bitter for Peter by the fact that Mr Kirkwood was a fellow Socialist. Yes, it was nasty, the whole episode. And I've often wondered how much courage it required for Peter to go on speaking about Animal Rights, when he was invariably subjected to fifth-rate satire for his pains from his colleagues on both sides of the House. But, then, he'd had plenty of practice at coping with first-rate satire in the form of his brother Arnold's 'Black Books'. And, in any case, he could always find consolation in the assurances of Sir Robert Gower, the Conservative MP who had been a guest at his vegetarian dinner and was Chairman of the RSPCA, not to mention the fighting marquis, and Ella.

Another attack on Peter was to become a source of pride, because it appeared in *Truth*, an untruthful journal that supported Sir Oswald Mosley when he left the Labour Party and founded the British Union of Fascists. An active supporter of this journal was the Deputy Director of MI5, a secret Nazi sympathiser, who retired in haste after Churchill became Prime Minister in 1940.

'The question of whether or not Parliament is losing its prestige is a favourite topic of conversation,' said *Truth* in May, 1930. 'And on the whole the "ayes" have it. Mr Peter Freeman, Labour MP for Brecon and Radnor, is one of those responsible for this phenomenon. He has suggested that no schoolchild should receive corporal punishment until he had had a 'kind of trial'. There was no hint as to what form this trial should take, or by whom it should be conducted. In any case, such details are not necessary because of the sheer fatuity of which Mr Freeman's constituents must be very ashamed. As, however, he is a non-smoker, teetotaller, vegetarian and a Theosophist, they are, perhaps, inured to his oddities by now'.

But the greatest oddity of all, it would seem, was his concern for suffering, human as well as animal. And in this respect, it has to be admitted that *Truth* was closer to the truth than some of Peter's other critics, who claimed that all he thought about was animals. In July, 1930, Hansard contained a report of his question to the Secretary of State for India, Mr Wedgewood Benn, who had been his rival for the Labour candidacy at Brecon and Radnor. Peter asked him about the injury done by police in Bombay to 'unarmed and non-violent citizens, particularly women and children,' who were demonstrating in favour of independence from Britain. And a year later, the *Express* reported that Peter was to ask the President of the Board of Education whether his attention had been called to the case of Doreen Fowler – aged 11 of Pengam in South Wales – who was struck with a cane by a man teacher 'for hanging about after school hours'.

These are just two out of many examples – from that period alone – of Peter's concern for his fellow human beings. And the following is just one out of many more examples – also from that period alone – of Ella's untiring support for Peter's work. 'Cefn Coed Labour Party Women's Section' was a heading in the *Express* for July 31st, 1931. And this is the story underneath:

'Members of this section were guests at Rectory Road in Penarth on Tuesday. After being taken there by coach from Breconshire, the ladies enjoyed an excellent lunch provided by Mrs Freeman. And during the afternoon a variety of games and competions, organised and directed by their hostess, kept the party in good spirits. Prizes were then awarded and a delicious tea was subsequently given on the lawn. Mrs Freeman was presented with a bouquet of carnations.'

How many votes was that worth, I wonder? And how appreciative was Peter when he was away from home, dealing with the two great issues of the day, peace and unemployment? Week after week, the *Express* published resolutions in favour of peace at meetings all over the constituency; at the Baptist Union, at the League of Nations Union – a voluntary support group – and at Labour Party branches, to name just a few. And in case a rumour should begin to spread that it was only naive persons in airy-fairy organisations who cared about peace, a letter was sent to the *Express* by Mr David Evans – a Tory, no less – who claimed that 'under the late Conservative government this country was actually leading the whole world in the direction of disarmament by example'. But at the same time, Hitler was spreading a message of hate in Germany and the Japanese were advancing from Korea into north-east China, regardless of what they said in Brecon and Radnor. Or anywhere else, if it comes to that. And from America came a popular song that was a cry of despair, brought about by unemployment – 'Buddy, Can You Spare a Dime?'

People felt themselves to be at the mercy of forces that were beyond the control not just of themselves, but of their governments, and perhaps even of their God – a truly cosmic fear. Edith Thomas, a 19-year-old woman from Crickhowell, might have been much more sensitive to it than most, and less capable of escaping from it mentally, and therefore more at risk. 'Woman's Body in Usk' was how the *Express* reported this tragedy; 'Her shopping was found on the river bank'.

A look at some of the headlines that confronted people who

read the newspapers might help us to understand what could have been the final straw for that poor woman – 'Dire Warnings on Economy'; 'Worsening Trade Figures'; 'Growing Unemployment'; and 'the Road to Ruin'. The first of these is from an editorial in the *County Times* about a speech by Mr Lansbury, First Commissioner of Works, at a Socialist Summer School in August, 1930. 'Mr Lansbury prefaced his remarks with an amiable observation that some of his hearers would probably want to boil him alive', said this editorial. 'We express no opinion on that point, though we think that the First Commissioner is in no immediate danger. His fellow Socialist, Mr Peter Freeman, who has been attempting for some time to stir public opinion on the subject of boiling lobsters in the House of Commons kitchen, would surely display an equal solicitude for so old and respected a Socialist as Mr Lansbury'.

It must have been irresistible – but it was also inexcusable – for the *County Times* to take a swipe at Peter, while reporting a speech that dealt with the problems of young men and young women who were living on public assistance, or no assistance at all, except from their parents.

One of the few people who seemed to be coping with the Great Depression was an old tramp – a gentleman of the road – who was found guilty by the magistrates in Knighton, Radnorshire, of 'fraudently obtaining relief' at the local Workhouse. 'He had his tea,' wrote the crime reporter of the *Express*. 'And afterwards, the Master asked him if he had any money to disclose. He said he had only fourpence, but on searching him, the Master found seven one pound notes, one ten shilling note, six shillings in silver and three pence in copper. Fined ten shillings'. He was a very naughty tramp, of course, but he must have got away with it before – in Workhouses across the land – or he would surely have taken the trouble to hide the cash before presenting himself for his free tea at Knighton.

Up in London, there was someone who paid a much higher price than a mere ten bob. He paid with his reputation. On August 27th, 1931, a Court Circular announced that the King had held a Conference at which the following were present – Mr J. Ramsay MacDonald, Prime Minister and Leader of the Labour Party; Mr Stanley Baldwin, Leader of the Opposition and of the Conservative Party; and Sir Herbert Samuel, representing the Liberals in place of Mr David Lloyd George, who was ill. Ramsay MacDonald offered his resignation as Prime Minister, which the King accepted. He, the King, then asked him to form a National Administration, which Mr MacDonald accepted; hoping to deal with the Great Depression by combining the talents of all three parties. It was not to be, because very few of his former colleagues were prepared to support him. He became, instead, a Socialist Prime Minister who was kept in power by Conservatives. Within hours, this National Government was denounced by the whole Labour Movement, including the vast majority of its MP's. And Ramsay MacDonald had become a traitor for the second time in his life. In 1914, he had been condemned as a traitor for opposing the war, which made him a hero of the Left. In 1931, he was condemned as a traitor by the Left for doing what he thought was necessary for the country at another time of crisis. He was collaborating with the enemy again – only this time, it wasn't the enemy of Britain, but of the Working Class. The new Leader of the Labour Party – and therefore of the Opposition – was to be

George Lansbury, a Christian gentleman, if ever there was one. But no match for the dictators who were coming to power all over Europe.

Peter fell into line with the Labour Movement's policy immediately. But he never laced his speeches with the ugly abuse that so many of his colleagues indulged themselves in, aping the so-called patriots of 1914 but using a different rhetoric. Peter's attitude was more sorrowful than angry. He still referred to his former leader as a 'Socialist,' and prefaced his name with a respectful 'Mr'. In other words, his attitude was the same as the Secretary of the Police and Prison Officers' Union, who had defended Mr MacDonald in 1914.

A National Government was probably inevitable, but what a pity it was that Stanley Baldwin didn't become Prime Minister, with Ramsay MacDonald as Leader of the Opposition, critical, supportive, and wise. It would have saved a lot of unnecessary suffering, for himself and for his Party. Labour was reduced from 287 to 52 members of parliament at the election in October, 1931, with Peter losing his seat to Captain Hall, an ardent supporter of a man he had previously despised.

There was to be no dancing this time, not for Peter, and no pretty girls. Because, after all, there was nothing to celebrate. His supporters sang to him instead – 'For He's a Jolly Good Fellow!' followed by three rousing cheers, which was no more than he deserved, because he had been a good constituency MP; one of the best, as testified by the letters which he wrote to people in trouble, touchingly preserved in the scrap-books and family-albums that were shown to me by their children.

A week or two later he went off to India as Chairman of the

Commonwealth of India League, leaving Ella to prepare for Christmas. It was to be a nice holiday for him; a period of recuperation before his forthcoming battles in another constituency. Against an opponent who lacked the advantages in life that were enjoyed by D'Arcy Hall; but was all the more dangerous because of it. He was lucky as well – phenomenally so – which meant that Peter had a fight on his hands.

Chapter 9

Enter the Two Reginalds

THE FIRST OF THESE REGINALDS was every bit as staunch a Tory as D'Arcy Hall, in spite of being educated at a technical college instead of Eton. And he wasn't just staunch, he was legendary – in the country at large, as well as in his own party – because he was credited with having brought about the downfall of a prime minister on the very day of his election as MP for Newport. He also played a respectable game of golf and enjoyed a beer or two, all of which was to make him a much more formidable opponent for Peter to deal with than Captain Hall had been. Peter was a bit of a legend himself, having been described to me by more than one person as a 'Scarlet Pimpernel' for his activities in Central Europe on the eve of World War Two. Especially in the city of Vienna – then under Nazi control – where he was to begin the romance that brought him tragedy as well as joy. But this was still in the future, whereas Reginald Clarry was in possession of his reputation already, when Peter was challenging him at the General Election of 1935.

So what exactly was this reputation? And how fully was it deserved?

Well, first of all, it must be said that it was certainly believed by a great many people in Newport, who in previous elections had voted for him in their tens of thousands, with the rallying cry of 'Good old Clarry!' One of these electors was so carried away that she painted the exterior of her house with the true-blue colour of Conservatism, from top to bottom. And this was in Pill, the docklands area, which might reasonably have been regarded as Peter Freeman country – the bastion of all that was red, the people's colour. The one thing that Peter could be said to have in his favour – apart from the other Reginald – was his bank balance, which enabled him to make substantial donations to Labour's electoral funds. But what good was that against a whole party whose balances were more than adequate, and which was led by a legendary figure?

The legend had endured since the 18th of October, 1922, because that was the day when Reginald Clarry first became the town's MP in a by-election conducted under intense scrutiny from the entire national press, not least from *The Times* of London. And the prime minister whose downfall he was said to have brought about – on that very same day – was none other than David Lloyd George, who had led the country to victory in 1918; and who would be a strong contender for the title of 'Greatest Ever Welshman'.

This Newport by-election had been seen by one and all as a test of that very peculiar entity, the Coalition Government, which – like the National Government of Ramsay MacDonald – was kept in power by Conservatives, while being led by a prime minister from a different party, in this case Lloyd George, who was a Liberal. It had been brought into existence by another Liberal prime minister, Henry Asquith, who possessed a satisfactory Liberal majority, but wanted a united parliament on his side to fight the war. That was in 1915. A year later, Lloyd George had taken over as Prime Minister, splitting the Liberal Party in the process; and he fought the General Election of 1918 as leader of this coalition of Tories and supportive Liberals. He was returned as the saviour of the nation, with a huge majority, more Conservative than before, though their leader was just as Liberal as ever. Very peculiar inded!

This is where Reginald Clarry comes in, together with the legend that was to surround him like an aura. Most of those Tories who had supported the Coalition at the Election of 1918 were becomming more than a little disenchanted by 1921. This applied mainly to the groundlings on the backbenches; but even some of the Tory ministers were murmuring and muttering about an arrangement that seemed to benefit no-one apart from Lloyd George. And by 1922 they were becoming downright mutinous. So much so that they had arranged a meeting to consider the whole question of their loyalty to this coalition, with its artful Liberal leader. And it was to take place at the salubrious venue of the Carlton Club – where else? – on the day that followed the by-election in Newport. The gentlemen who attended this meeting were hoping that Reginald Clarry would win, because he was as strongly opposed to the coalition as they were. But they weren't expecting him to. All the commentators believed it would be won by the Labour candidate; a worthy man, but not dynamic like Peter.

So far so good. We have only had to tell one story. But from now on, it must be two. First of all, there's the story that made Mr Clarry a legend; which his supporters in Newport were to believe forever afterwards. And not just his supporters; everyone. According to this version, the Tory MP's had gathered at the Carlton Club in a gloomy frame of mind, which couldn't even be lifted by the odd glass of champers or of Highland Malt. They fully expected a Conservative defeat at Newport. And a victory at their meeting for the abominable Coalition, which would be brought about – they believed – by a series of passionate speeches from their party leaders, with their seats in Lloyd George's cabinet. But then – lo and behold! – a messenger arrived with the news that Reginald Clarry had won at Newport, a stunning victory for a sworn enemy of the Coalition. There was loud cheering, naturally, followed by more orders for the waiters, after which the end of the Coalition was as certain as anything could be. All it needed was the formality of a vote in the Commons.

That, then, was the legend, so very beneficial to Reginald Clarry. In reality, the Newport result was announced at 2.00 in the morning, from the steps of Newport Town Hall, a good nine hours before the disgruntled Tories had begun to arrive at their meeting, which was expected to end the Coalition anyway. But what earthly use was this sober truth in comparison with that glorious legend, especially when it came to a contest against a man whose reputation was that of a campaigner for lost causes.

Lost causes? Downright bad ones, more like. He was a representative of the Theosophical Society on a local committee that was campaigning for the abolition of capital punishment, which was all very well when it came to crimes of passion, such as a jealous husband who kills his wife in a fit of rage for going to bed with a lover. But what do you make of a man who buries a baby alive? Such a case was reported in the *South Wales Argus* in 1935, the year when Peter was to challenge that knight in shining armour, Good old Clarry. At the General Election. And the *South Wales Argus* – which I'll call the *Argus* from now on – would be reporting the election as the paper for Newport, the only one. And it wasn't a Labour paper, either; not by any stretch of the imagination. It wasn't even Welsh, despite the 'South Wales' of its title. But even this would benefit Reginald Clarry more than Peter – as I'll explain – though both of them were English. It must be said, however, that the *Argus* wasn't like the *Brecon County Times*. It was as fair as it could possibly have been, given its outlook.

The *Argus* wasn't Welsh, because Newport wasn't Welsh – not really. The town was thoroughly confused, or open-minded, depending on your point of view. Even its accent is confused, being a mixture of Welsh and West Country English, the result of a massive immigration into South Wales from Somerset and Gloucestershire towards the end of the 19th century, including some of my own forebears; the ones who provided me with the name of Bloxsome. Schools in Newport in Peter's time could take a day off for both St David and St George. What could be more open-minded than that? Or more confused? Then there was the case of Ernie Hammett, one of Newport's greatest sporting heroes, who played football for Wales against England in 1912 as a centre forward, and rugby for England against Wales in 1920 as a centre-threequarter. One final example is Aneurin Bevan, creator of the NHS, who might well be thought of as a rival to Lloyd George for the title of 'Greatest Ever Welsman'. Even he was confused about his Celtic idenity, though he wasn't actually from Newport, but from a valley outside. On March 31st, 1951, the *Argus* carried a statement from Mr Bevan, complaining that the Tredegar Orpheus Male Voice Choir – of which he was President – would be unable to compete at the National Eisteddfod of Wales, because of having to sing in Welsh. 'I think,' he was quoted as saying, 'that the Eisteddfod authorities are showing a lamentable tendency towards bigotry'.

'Bigotry'? What a charge to make, when Paul Robeson from America had gone to the trouble, years before, of learning a song in Welsh, to sing at the Miners' Eisteddfod in Porthcawl.

But there was one respect in which Newport and the valleys outside were very definitely Welsh, much to the annoyance of their inhabitants – or the men amongst them, at any rate. By law, the pubs were closed on a Sunday, like everywhere else in Wales. It had already been an issue at the by-election in 1922 – a year which is remembered by every Conservative MP who ever attends the '1922 Committee', a meeting of his party's backbenchers – adding something else to the aura that Reginald Clarry seemed to carry around with him. He had opposed the Sunday-Closing Law as part of his campaign at that famous election, and was still opposing it in 1935 – winning a lot of very active support from the Licensed Victuallers Association – whereas Peter was a teetotaller, the subject of a many a hearty joke in the pubs of Newport.

And to make matters worse – or more confusing for the voter – from the time he had moved to Penarth, where he continued to live, he had developed a fondness for all things Welsh; had 'gone native,' you might say. This would not have been so bad if it had been restricted to supporting the Welsh rugby team, which Peter undoubtedly did, but it went much further, I'm afraid. As MP for Brecon and Radnor, he had suggested to the Prime Minister, Ramsay MacDonald, that Wales should have a powerful voice in the cabinet, a Secretary of State. He'd also written a book, if you please! – *The Druids And Theosophy* – that contained a great many statements in praise of those ancient bearers of Celtic wisdom;

though most of the people in Newport would have regarded them as very strange men in stranger attire, who sought favours from the gods by sacrificing virgins on slabs of stone without so much as a 'by your leave'.

In some respects, then, Peter was his own worst enemy for espousing causes which the voters of Newport considered peculiar, if not downright weird. Whereas 'good old Clarry' was as normal a man as you could wish for. But this had been the situation in Brecon and Radnor – more or less – when Peter had managed to win.

So what was the state of the parties in the run up to the election of 1935? Much the same as in 1931, actually. The Government was still calling itself 'National,' though it was now being led by Stanley Baldwin, a Conservative whose son was standing for Labour – this was Oliver Baldwin, a friend of Peter's, who had spoken for him at Brecon and Radnor. The Opposition was still Labour, still the same, except for its leader – who was no longer Mr Lansbury, the pacifist, but Major Attlee, using his rank from the First World War; possibly as an indication that he was not to be regarded as a soft touch when it came to dealing with the likes of Hitler or Mussolini. And what about the issues? Well, a couple of quotations from the *Argus* will show that they, too, were much the same as in 1931. In January, 1935, there was an alarming headline, especially for those who lived alone – 'Slump's Effect On Young Men: House Breaking'. And a week or two later, there was a headline that can only be described as deeply sinister – 'Saar Jews Tremble After Sweeping German Vote,' it said. 'New Exodus Of Hebrews'. The Saar was a part of Rhineland Germany which had been under League of Nations control since 1918, the idea being that its coal should go to France as compensation for the destruction of her mines by the German army. And the debt having been paid, its inhabitants had decided by referendum to become a part of the Fatherland again. The Jews who lived in the Saar would, therefore, be treated in exactly the same way as in the rest of Germany. They would be deprived of their citizenship – even of their humanity – in the search for some more permament solution to the problem of their existence.

But the desire of everyone in Britain was for peace and a return to prosperity. David Morgan of Cardiff, a department store, was tempting the women readers of various papers – including the *Argus* – with 'Stylish Frocks For Less Than Eleven Shillings'. And the Reverend Dick Shepherd was founding his Peace Pledge Union. How, I wonder, could he have reconciled this commendable activity with standing up to Hitler in defence of those 'Hebrews' who were trembling? Or the women who bought those stylish frocks, regarding them as an absolute bargain... Did they give so much as a thought to the wives of the unemployed, who could only look at them in David Morgan's beautifully-appointed windows? Not even that, if they couldn't afford the bus fare to Cardiff.

The first of Newport's contestants to come out of his corner was Reginald Clarry, the champion. And it was obvious he was going to fight dirty, with no holds barred. Because if Newport could be Labour once – as it had been from 1929 to 1931 – it could be Labour again.

'I maintain in all seriousness,' he said – according to a report in the *Argus* – 'that this is the cleverest political document since Rousseau and Voltaire, whose writings led up to the

French Revolution!'

He was referring to the Manifesto that had been published by the Labour Party, which was still being tarred – as at Brecon and Radnor – with the Jacobin brush, ready and willing to set up a guillotine, anywhere and everywhere. In Somerton Park, for example – Newport's football ground – where the spectators would have plenty of room to enjoy a picnic; while the heads were dropping nicely into the basket, beginning with Mr Clarry's. Then he went on to have a dig at Peter himself, because of his love for India, and his support for its independence from Britain. 'We must see that there is no question of any break up in our great empire,' said Mr Clarry – apparently unafraid that he might end up without a head for these critical remarks – and implying that to give the Indians their independence would be as callous as putting one's elderly parents into a Residential Home.

But Peter had learned a thing or two during his time at Brecon and Radnor – some ring craft – making him more than capable of dealing with an opponent, however dirty the fight. 'Mr Clarry claims to have attended every Parliamentary Division of importance to Newport,' he said at one of his own public meetings, also reported in the *Argus*. 'Well, I have the records with me now. Last year Mr Clarry was absent from 269 Divisions out of a possible 414. These Divisions included the manufacture of armaments – a Newport industry – the Means Test for the unemployed, and Electoral Reform' – the latter being important as regards the Sunday opening of pubs. And Ella supported him at this meeting by saying, 'I have never made a political speech in my life. Anyone who votes for my husband will never regret it'.

Which means, I believe, that Peter was ahead on points; because the support of one's family counts for a lot at an election. As does the timely intervention of a heckler at the meeting of an opponent, something which the papers love – whatever side the heckler might be on. In the later stages of the campaign, Mr Clarry was claiming that 'During the last four years a million more men had been found jobs'.

'In Training Centres!' bellowed someone who was described in the *Argus* as 'a voice'. He meant, of course, that they weren't 'proper' jobs.

'Don't talk nonsense!' bellowed Reginald back to him. But the fact that he couldn't think of anything more cutting shows that he was rattled.

And Peter was able to benefit still further from this 'voice' by stating subsequently that 'the National Government claims to have reduced the unemployment figures by a million. Half of that number had been taken from the Unemployment Register and placed on the Public Assistance Register'.

On November 9th – less than a week before polling day – there was a photograph in the *Argus* of Peter and Reginald together, immediately after the nomination ceremonies at the Town Hall. And Peter is undoubtedly the smarter of the two – in his usual white suit for election time, but on this occasion with a walking stick, which in 1935 was considered the height of fashion. It was this picture that caused me to dream about my subject for the one and only time: I was at his house in Penarth where everything was as white as that suit, including the furniture. 'I believe you're writing my biography,' said Peter, suddenly appearing.

'Yes, I am,' I replied.

'Well, I've got some letters here that would interest you.'

Then he disappeared, just as I was hoping that they might have been from a woman, since I didn't yet know of any definite affair, only of rumours.

There was someone else in that photograph, too – the second of the Reginalds, who ought to have been introduced to you long ago, as he was Peter's agent in Newport, already hard at work for him. In his way, he was every bit as interesting a character as Tudor Watkins – possibly more so – but he never became an MP himself, or a Lord, as Tudor did. Also, he preferred to be called 'Reg', which is convenient for distinguishing him from his Tory namesake; though before very long, we'll have to stop calling the other Reginald 'Reginald'; because in 1936, he was knighted, becoming Sir Reginald instead.

But we'd better go back to the election campaign of 1935, while promising to explain in the next chapter why Reg Ley – to give you his name in full – was such a remarkable man; unique, his friends claimed, in the whole of history – and they were right.

When he was announcing the date of the election, Mr Baldwin had said, 'I will not be responsible for the conduct of of any government in this country if I am not given power to remedy those deficiencies that have occurred in our defence services since the war'. But he added that he was prepared to follow a policy of peace 'with all my heart and soul'. This was a carefully measured statement from the Front Bench in the House of Commons, but the same ambiguity towards defence – brought about by memories of 1914 to 1918, combined with fear of what Hitler and Mussolini were up to – was to be found everywhere in the country. And it is here that Peter might have lost a round or two on points to his rival. Mr Clarry maintained that military force – 'being prepared,' as he called it – 'will give us a stronger voice in the League of Nations'. Whereas Peter stated the pacifist case, pure and simple, blotting out that youthful indiscretion with the London Scottish Rifle Volunteers. 'I stand on the side of peace,' he said, unequivocally, 'and I shall make every effort to reduce our armaments'.

Polling started at 7.00 a.m. on November 14th, with the *Argus* reporting that housewives 'took the opportunity of voting early, and then returned home to prepare the mid-day meal'. It was a terrible day –'wet and gloomy' – but that didn't stop the oldest elector from voting, nor the youngest. They were photographed together outside the Polling Station – Mr W. E. Heard, who was a hundred, and John Angus Evans, who was accompanied by his mother, being only seven. Apparently, anyone whose name was on the Register of Electors was entitled to vote, even if it was there by mistake. And when an *Argus* reporter called at the youngest elector's home for an interview, his mother said that it wouldn't be possible, not just then – because he was 'out playing'.

The election results in the *Argus* were close to an intriguing headline that said 'Lady Tavistock And Children's Tutor'. But the case – brought, of course, by Lord Tavistock – was passing through one of its less intriguing phases, which made it easier to find out what had happened to Peter, and without delay. He lost, though by less than 2,000 votes, which wasn't bad. Mr Clarry accounted for his success by saying that 'Newport has again shown common sense and judgement'. Peter blamed his failure on the town being flooded with cars belonging to 'wealthy people,' while the Labour Party 'had but few'. It might also be the case that Peter had been over-optimistic about the prospects for peace, much more optimistic than his party leader, Major Attlee, whereas Reginald Clarry had got it just about right, with his 'being prepared' – the Boy Scouts' motto, more or less. Mr Baldwin remained as Prime Minister and Major Attlee as Leader of the Opposition.

With no parliamentary duties to attend to, Peter learned to fly an aeroplane. But more importantly for his future – and for that of his entire family – he made a tour of Nazi central Europe as General Secretary of the Theosophical Society in Wales. It was a prolonged tour that included a visit to the enchanting city of Vienna, which was to earn for him his reputation as a Scarlet Pimpernel. And after returning home, there was a silver wedding to celebrate, his and Ella's. They received a great many gifts, not least of which was a 'beautiful coffee tray, duly inscribed' – presented to them by their fellow Theosophists in Wales; the people whom Peter had so recently been representing in the City of Dreams – and of the Gestapo.

Chapter 10

Pacifists at War

A N ELECTION AGENT is much the same as a butler, but instead of being a gentleman's gentleman, he's a polititician's politician, often more adroit than his master, and there weren't many who were as good at it as Reg Ley, although he didn't look the part. He wore glasses, to start off with, and he was powerfully built, having served his time both as a carpenter and as a convict in the toughest prison of them all – Dartmoor. But he could be as smooth as Jeeves himself when the occasion demanded, as it did in 1944, with Churchill firmly in control as leader of the Wartime Coalition, as well as the Conservative Party.

Not long after the Normandy landings, a meeting of Newport Labour Party's Executive Committee passed an apparently harmless-sounding resolution: 'It is recommended that Mr Freeman be asked to meet the Finance Committee at the earliest possible date'. Did I say 'harmless'? Well, not for Peter, who would obviously be asked for money – and plenty of it – now that victory was close in the war against Nazism, together with the election that would be called immediately afterwards; and not for Reg, either, who would have the ticklish job of going to Penarth and telling Peter what was expected of him, over the vegetarian cutlets and the nut roast. In particular, he would need to remind Peter of the £100 that he had promised for the Election Fund – up front, as they say – and of the not inconsiderable amounts that he had promised to pay annually, whether an election was in the offing or not.

If there was anyone with both the guile and the finesse to ask for money, that person was Reg Ley, but not for himself, of course: only for his Party or his God. He was one of nature's idealists, who had declared himself a Conscientious Objector in the First World War, and had been registered as such on the grounds of his 'international socialist principles', which meant that he wanted the working classes in every land to build a better future for themselves, instead of killing each other at the behest of their so-called superiors. And he refused point-blank to be called upon for any alternative to military service – like forestry or mining – on the grounds that he would still be assisting the warmongers. This wasn't an easy decision for a married man to take – especially one with children – since it meant prison, first at Wormwood Scrubs, then Wakefield, and finally, Dartmoor. The only comfort for Reg in all of this – but what a comfort it proved to be! – was that his wife had come to share his views about the war, because of her deep religious convictions.

When he arrived at Dartmoor – all the way from Wakefield in Yorkshire, with several changes of train and handcuffed to a warder – he was told he could have a book from the prison library; a very real pleasure for someone who was already an avid reader, having worked his way through that classic of literature and of scholarship, Gibbon's *Decline And Fall Of The Roman Empire*, all six volumes of it; something that many a history graduate has never managed to do – myself included, I'm sorry to say. But the book they gave him was *A Healthy Home And How To Keep It*, followed by a school history reader for ten-to-eleven year olds. Like everyone else, he did his share of cutting stones in a moorland quarry; though he was later given a clerical job, keeping a register of his fellow prisoners according to religious belief. One man told him, 'I'm a bloody atheist! But put me down as C. of E.' A very wise deception in Reg's opinion, because attendance at a religious service would earn him a glimpse of someone from outside the prison. Which could have been anyone at all. Even a woman, if he was lucky.

I said just now that Reg was one of nature's idealists. Well, that was certainly true. But he wasn't one of nature's ideologues, incapable of adapting his beliefs to a changing world. By 1939, he had ceased to be a pacifist – at least temporarily – as had so many others. Including Bertrand Russell, that naughty philosopher, and Albert Einstein, who had opposed the war of 1914 to 1918 from the opposite side – from Berlin, where he was completing his masterpiece, the General Theory of Relativity. Reg was a civil defence worker in Newport for the whole of the Second World War, a full-time professional. Because of this – and because of his experience as an agent for Peter – he was asked in 1946 to become a United Nations Observer at the elections in Greece, which was in the throes of a civil war between Communist and Anti-Communist forces. Reg's colleagues – a Frenchman and an American – were generals; people of considerable status, so the new Labour government in London made him equal to them by giving him the rank of Brigadier for the duration of his UN appointment. Reg could therefore claim to be the only pacifist who ever became a general, and possibly the only convict.

The Minutes of Newport Labour Party's Executive Committee are often very sad from 1939 to 1945; as, I expect, are those of the Conservatives and Liberals. On July 21st, 1944, 'A vote of condolence was passed for Councillor Mrs Gibbons on the death of her son in action'. And at the same meeting, 'A vote of sympathy was extended to Councillor Telling on hearing that his son had been wounded'.

A couple of items from the *Argus* will explain as well as any history book why those very young men had to suffer in battle – one of them mortally – and why Reg had abandoned his pacifism. The first of these items deals with Hitler's reaction to an attempt on his life in the July Conspiracy of 1944, when a time-bomb in a brief-case was put close to him by Count von Stauffenberg at the army headquarters in East Prussia. Referring to his survival, which the Nazis described as 'miraculous,' he said in a broadcast to the German people, 'I regard it as a confirmation of the task imposed on me by Providence' – which is a perfect expression of all that is meant by the word 'fanatical,' especially when you remember that his 'task' included the extermination of entire peoples and the enslavement of others. The second item – also from 1944 – concerns a concert to be held in Ebbw Vale to raise money for 'comforts' as they were called, little treats for men at the front, such as a packet of cigarettes or a bottle of beer – possibly the last they would ever enjoy. But the Lord's Day Observance Society objected to this concert on the grounds that it was to be held on a Sunday, when all right-thinking people should be on their knees, praying – including, presumably, the soldiers at the front. Can you imagine such an objection being allowed by Hitler? Or if it comes to that, by Goebbels, Hitler's Minister of Propaganda (though he preferred the word 'enlightenment') who was claiming that 'within a reasonable time we shall have completely regained the initiative' – more than a year after the defeat at Stalingrad, and within months of the Normandy Landings.

It was a war against the forces of unreason, which had included Italy until it went over to the Allied side in October, 1943, after the fall of Mussolini. And that meant questions at Westminster about the Italian prisoners-of-war in Britain, who were now no longer prisoners, but allied soldiers – and could not, therefore, be confined to their camps. More than one MP made a complaint to the Home Secretary that former Italian prisoners were roaming around at all hours, making merry with the local women: which brings us back to Peter.

As already stated, he had been travelling before the war in those parts of Europe that were already under Nazi control, including Vienna, where he embarked on the one affair of his life which blossomed into romance. I was told by several people that the woman in question was Jewish, and might well have gone to Auschwitz – then to a gas chamber – if Peter hadn't smuggled her across the border into Switzerland under the very noses of the Gestapo; thus earning for himself the title of 'Scarlet Pimpernel'. On further investigation, it turned out that this story was a fantasy, created by his admirers in Newport; which is a pity, I suppose; though the actual one is just as extraordinary, and in some ways at least, just as flattering to Peter; though it will have to wait until a later chapter, where it fits in better.

In his report for 1940 as Secretary of the Theosophical Society in Wales, Peter says that 'Britain now stands alone as the bulwark of justice and freedom amongst the fighting nations of the world. Quiet confidence and loyal comradeship must be maintained until a new day shall dawn and Mankind reaches a higher step on the ladder of evolution'.

Winston Churchill himself might well have used those very words – apart, that is, from the ones about a 'ladder of evolution,' which were meant for Theosophists alone. Peter was saying in effect that he had been forced to abandon his pacifism, as Reg Ley had done; and David, too – Peter's son – whose war I shall describe in a minute or so, the most exciting of them all. In his report for 1942, Peter demonstrates the meaning of Democracy in much the same way as the Lord's Day Observance Society in Ebbw Vale – by criticising his own side, war or no war. Referring to India, he says, 'Let us trust that ways will be found for applying the principles of the Atlantic Charter to this great nation forthwith': independence, that is – without delay, and implying that it should have happened sooner.

In another report – the one for 1944 – he tells the members of his resignation from the job of Secretary, saying that the post-war election will demand every ounce of his energy. But to show there's no ill-feeling, he composes a limerick for them, a theosophical one, which goes as follows:

> There's a cheery old fellow of Burma
> Who says, 'Against fate I don't murmer.
> For whatever you get
> In this life, you can bet
> That it's all in accordance with Karma!'

If Reg could claim to have been the only pacifist who ever became a general, Peter could make an equally spectacular claim – that he had changed from a pacifist to an arms manufacturer; which is roughly equivalent to the Queen becoming a dinner lady, and the Pope an atheist – or even a protestant! But Peter wasn't ashamed of his conversion. Why should he be? If the war was to be fought, it had to be fought properly. You couldn't face a Panzer Division with placards saying, 'NAZIS OUT!' And he didn't make the same mistake as at Brecon and Radnor – where he tried to hide his pacifism by mentioning his brief flirtation with militarism in the London Scottish Rifle Volunteers. In Newport, he made it quite plain that he wasn't a pacifist – for the time being, at any rate – by declaring openly that he was a director of several armaments companies – manufacturing, amongst other things, the magnetos for fighter planes and the tails for mortar bombs. And it might have been this which accounted for the rumour that he had fallen in love with a Jewish girl, whom he had ghosted away from the nightmare that was Nazism. One of the companies he was involved with had been founded by a Jewish refugee family called Diss – Austrian Jews at that – to whom Peter had lent a lot of money and a lot of support. Mr Diss, the father of this family, had learnt his English from the employees at his Cardiff factory – including their term for nuts with wings on, 'those winged bastards', which he used in a letter to the suppliers, who were regular chapel goers, renowned for their piety.

One of the nicest documents I've come across in all of my research for this book was the account by David Freeman – Peter's son – of his time in the army, which he wrote for a girl called Genna at the local Comprehensive School, who wanted it for a project on the Second World War. I'll summarise it for you now, as I did with his grandmother's story about that 'Dreadful Year,' when all of her family were ill.

'On the 17th of October, 1940, I was called up into the army,' he says. 'I had been a pacifist and a vegetarian, and neither of these fitted me for the army, but I polished my boots and I had the right accent so I was sent to be trained as an officer and became a Second Lieutenant … In 1941 I was posted to Singapore by ship, a journey which took seventeen weeks round by Cape Town in South Africa…'

I'll have to interrupt every now and again to make a connection where I've left something out; this is the first of them: they must have sent him via Cape Town – instead of the Suez Canal – because of the fighting in North Africa, and he arrived in Singapore not long before the Japanese, who brought about 'the worst disaster in British military history,' as Churchill called it. They were commanded by the notorious General Yamashita, later to be hanged as a war criminal. But meanwhile, before the Japanese had occupied the part of Singapore where David was, he and two other officers decided to look for a boat in which to escape.

'I had kept my tommy gun and my army compass,' he continues. 'Also, when staying in an empty house I had found a child's *Atlas of the World*, and had torn out the page which showed Singapore… Later we found a warehouse full of cases of food and drink… And while looking for a boat we met up with a group of British Commandos, led by a major, who had already found one… It was a Chinese junk, with one mast and one square sail… We brought them some cases of food from the warehouse… and just as they were going – without us! – I produced my little map and my army compass and asked whether they could squeeze the three of us on board. They were crowded already but agreed. There were now 36 of us on board, with just enough room to sit squashed up round the edge, with the food piled in the middle…'

Among all those on the junk not one had ever learned to sail before. Now their lives depended on this 'unwieldy contraption,' together with a page from a child's atlas.

'In Singapore town the oil refinery had been set on fire, and the whole sky was dark with smoke... this gave us some cover as we sailed out of the harbour and towards Sumatra ...

'Afraid of being spotted by the Japanese who might machine-gun us from their planes, we sailed only by night, and at dawn pulled the junk into one of the hundreds of little islands that we saw, none of which was marked on the map, so small was the scale...

'The commando major had lots of money, so if we needed supplies, we could buy them from the local inhabitants... We made camp fires and in a way enjoyed ourselves. After five days we reached Sumatra...'

In Sumatra they threw away their army uniforms, which were stinking, flea-infested rags by then, and they bought the clothes that the Sumatran people wore, nice and new and clean – a sarong, which is a sort of unisex skirt; a shirt; and a wide-brimmed straw hat. Some weeks later, they reached Bombay on the west coast of India, having hitched a lift aboard a passenger liner. After disembarking, they went for a celebratory meal to the best hotel in town, the Taj Mahal, still wearing their sarongs.

'Finally,' he says, 'I found myself in the Indian Army, with Indian troops... I got on well with them and learnt to speak Urdu. For three years I lived mainly in the jungle and never had any home leave. So you can imagine how I missed my parents!'

Just as good a storyteller as his grandmother, isn't he? Undoubtedly. But there was something he didn't mention to Genna, as it wouldn't have been relevant to her project. While he was still in the jungle, fighting the Japanese, David received a letter from home. It told him that in the County of Middlesex – far from the professional curiosity of reporters on the *Argus* or the *Penarth Times* – a judge of the High Court by the name of Sir Gonne Pilcher had decided to grant Ella a Decree Nisi, ending her marriage on the grounds of Peter's infidelity. David wasn't surprised, but he was still upset. These were the parents he loved and whom he missed – the mother who used to take him, as a little boy, on the paddle steamers that went from Penarth to Ilfracombe or Weston-super-Mare, the mother he adored. And the father with whom he had formed an unbeatable tennis doubles partnership, a very good father, too – whatever his shortcomings as a husband.

The news which that letter brought to David in the jungle was a fulfilment of the prophesy that Arnold had made in 1912, two years before Peter and Ella were even married. In his Black Book for that year, there's a drawing of Peter as an angel, supposedly executed by Annie Besant, the leader of world Theosophy. Beneath it are some words, again ascribed to Annie Besant – 'Peter isn't married, but his heart is another's'. Lastly, there's Peter's reply to his theosophical guru, the woman who had pictured him as an angel – 'I shall leave her later, but wed her now to work off coils and coils of cursed Karma!'

These coils would have to be worked off once again, with another woman – called Ellie, instead of Ella – but before that, there's the end of the war to be considered, and the 1945 Election – in both of which our hero was deeply involved.

Chapter 11

From Major to Mister

IF PROOF WERE NEEDED that the Battle of the Atlantic had been won – and won decisively – it was in the fact that from January 1945 onwards, people could have marmalade on their toast a couple of times a week, instead of just once. Allied merchant ships were not being sunk any longer by German submarines, and could therefore bring us oranges in greater quantities from the coasts of Africa, as well as the usual arms and ammunition from north America. The doubling of the marmalade ration had been reported in the *Argus*, which also informed its readers that consideration was being given to a peacetime project, the construction of a badly-needed bridge across the Severn. On the continent of Europe, Paris had already been liberated – months before – and the girls there were seen to be wearing lipstick again after all the shortages of the Occupation.

Then came the long-awaited announcement on the BBC that 'hostilities' – as they quaintly put it – would cease in Europe at one minute past midnight on the 9th of May, 1945, and the country went mad.

But, sadly, there was one person in our story who didn't live to enjoy these celebrations, or even his extra marmalade, if it came to that. At a meeting of the Newport Labour Party Executive in the previous January, there was just a single item under consideration: 'The situation which has been brought about by the death of Sir Reginald Clarry,' as they somewhat heartlessly expressed it. Being honourable people, however – despite this lapse into heartlessness – the meeting decided to abide by the terms of the wartime electoral pact, whereby all the main parties had agreed that they wouldn't fight any election until peace had come, but would allow the party of a deceased member to nominate a successor. The Newport Conservative Association nominated Lieutenant Commander Bell, RNVR (Royal Naval Volunteer Reserve). But he still had a fight on his hands, because the ILP (Independent Labour Party) decided to oppose him. The ILP had disaffiliated from the main party in 1932, and had not agreed to the wartime electoral pact. Perish the thought! So they put up a candidate with the undeniably proletarian name of Bob – Bob Edwards in full – which contrasted very nicely with the Lieutenant Commander in front of his opponent's name. As well as the officer-class initials after it.

Bob lost no time in telling the people of Newport that he would not stand by and allow their town to be 'thrown away to the Tories'. For good measure, he added that the whole of Britain was faced with 'the threat of dictatorship from the monopoly capitalists'. But he still lost, in spite of these dire prophesies, and in spite, also, of his generous offer to deal with the menace of capitalism on the voters' behalf. Single-handedly, if necessary – as St. George had dealt with the dragon. Lieutenant Commander Bell became the MP for Newport on Thursday, May 17th, 1945, just a week or so after the German generals had formally capitulated in the ancient city of Rheims, and a mere couple of months before he would have to fight another election, this time against our Peter.

As at Brecon and Radnor, there was first of all a rival to be vanquished from within the party itself; an army officer by the name of Roy Jenkins, who decades later was to abandon the Labour Movement and become – as Lord Hillhead – the leader of the Liberal Democrat Peers. There are two versions to the story of his attempt at taking over as candidate from Peter; his own, and that of the Labour veterans in Newport, who see him – naturally enough – as a traitor to their cause, a vile turncoat. They told me that he had got in touch with Reg Ley, suggesting that Peter's divorce, which he apparently described as 'messy', would not look good when the Tory Press got hold of it, and the consequence might be that Lieutenant Commander Bell would continue in the seat, possibly with an increased majority – especially as he was not given to philandering, despite the effect which his uniform, with all that gold braid, was having on the local girls. Then there is the version of the story that Lord Hillhead gave to me when I informed him, as tactfully as I could, about the views of those Labour veterans. As regards the lesser charge of attempting to replace Peter as the candidate, he told me, 'There is an element of truth in the story, though not more'. But as regards the greater charge, he denied it altogether: 'I would not have dreamt of trying to force Freeman out on account of his divorce', which makes it very difficult to come down on one side or the other. I found them equally convincing, the veterans and the noble lord, and equally unlikely to modify their point of view, with so much at stake – in one case, a much-loved ideal, and in the other, a jealously guarded reputation.

The Coalition Government – which included Major Attlee as Deputy Prime Minister – had resigned towards the end of May, though Mr Churchill agreed to form a purely Conservative administration for running the country until the General Election, which had been set for July. Clement Attlee became Leader of the Opposition once again, calling himself 'Mr' now, instead of 'Major,' another sign of peace. But there were still a great many causes for anxiety; not least of which was the continuing war against Japan in Asia, with reports of many casualties. At home, there were unexploded bombs – left over from German air raids or British army manoeuvres – that had sunk into the ground, waiting to be trodden on. The Gwent Coroner issued a warning against this hidden danger after some walkers had been killed by a blast on the Sugar Loaf, a mountain near Abergavenny.

But the forthcoming election was occupying more and more of people's attention, including that of children, who were composing their own up-to-date versions of the old electioneering songs, keeping them as bloodthirsty as ever. 'If it wasn't for your wife, we would stab you with a knife!' – that was the warning they issued to any candidate they disapproved of, regardless of marital status. And, sometimes, even of gender.

Newport Labour Party was fortunate that it didn't have a bank balance in the red, however appropriate the colour might have been for an organisation of the Left. At a meeting of the Executive on May18th, it was agreed unanimously that £40 should be donated 'forthwith' to the national fighting fund. A lot of money, when you consider that a pint of beer would have cost them less than a shilling, which means less than five pence. Reg Ley, as Secretary, made an appeal for at least twenty cars on Polling Day – at least, mind you! – in the Workers' Party: an indication that Labour was now attracting in greater numbers those affluent idealists who had previously been Liberal. The meeting also decided that a short-hand typist and a clerk would have to be employed 'for the duration of the campaign', full-time.

None of this was to absolve Peter from making his own financial contribution; with or without a little arm-twisting by Reg Ley, which might have been necessary because of that 'messy' and undoubtedly expensive divorce. The Executive knew in advance – from harsh experience – that all of their lovely bank balance would be swallowed up in the course of the election. Peter agreed to pay £100 into constituency funds when the election was over, to top them up again – plus £40 annually, should he be returned as member, in addition to everything else that he'd promised.

There were two brooding presences that hovered over the General Election of 1945, both of them a cause of much discomfort to Peter, as to every other Labour candidate in Britain. One of them was a Conservative, the great man who had led us to victory over Hitler, and who naturally expected to retain a home at Number Ten Downing Street. The other was Chairman of the Labour Party's National Executive Committee; a figure of dread to the Tory Press, more sinister in his way than Robespierre and Lenin put together. Peter also had to contend with anti-semitism – though he wasn't Jewish at all – and with accusations about his business practices; though not, oddly enough, about his sexual ones.

'There is a very general sentiment,' said Lieutenant Commander Bell – whom I shall refer to simply as 'Commander' from now on – 'that the leadership of Mr Churchill should continue'. The *Argus* put it even more strongly: in an editorial on Saturday, June 30th, headed 'Vote For Liberty,' it said that 'In this election we appeal for votes for Mr Winston Churchill. He is the towering personality in world politics to-day'. The *Argus* wasn't prejudiced against Peter, as the *Brecon County Times* had been. Not at all; it was reflecting what seemed to be the popular feeling, and the polite one. Because after all, how could you possibly get rid of Winston after he'd saved the country from Hitler? Utterly unthinkable!

Then there was that other bugbear for Labour – that other brooding presence – the Chairman of its own Executive Committee. This was Professor Harold Laski, a person of foreign extraction and, worse still, an intellectual, who wouldn't have been able – for the life of him – to tell you how Arsenal or Chelsea had got on in their previous match, let alone Newport County. The learned professor had written a book in 1935 – entitled *The State In Theory And Practice* – which was known to espouse a form of Marxism, the philosophy that motivated the Russian Revolution of October, 1917. Now, in post-war Britain there was a vogue for all things Russian, based on the undoubtedly heroic achievements of the Russian army. Even Joseph Stalin – their feared dictator – shared in this warmth towards his people, being known as 'Uncle Joe'. Hardly anyone, however, was as kindly disposed towards Uncle Joe's philosophy – towards Marxism – as Professor Laski apparently was, and if they had been, the bulk of the Press was ready to point out to them that it involved the abolition of everything private, down to their own little homes; and the most severe punishment for anyone who dared to speak their mind. This, of course, was exactly where Peter and his colleagues were at another disadvantage. They called themselves Socialists, as did the ruling elite in Russia. But what the Labour Party meant by Socialism was something entirely different, especially when it came to personal freedom. Their Socialism was gentle and democratic, owing more to the decencies of ordinary people than to the speculations of a philosopher, however well-read. Unfortunately, these subtleties were lost on anti-Labour speakers – or conveniently ignored by them – making it more than a little difficult for the Labour Party to live with the embarrassment that its own Chairman was causing.

The *Argus* reported Commander Bell as saying that 'the danger of voting Socialist was that if a Socialist majority were obtained, the elected government would be merely puppets in the hands of men like Professor Laski – unscrupulous backroom boys whose power would amount to a dictatorship'. Which is precisely how Stalin had become a dictator in Russia; because he had used his position as Communist Party Secretary – a backroom job – to learn about his rivals from their personal files in Moscow. He had then manipulated or eliminated them, according to what he had seen in these files – or promoted them, which meant buying them. And it wasn't only Commander Bell who made these allegations; they were all at it, including Mr Churchill himself, who wrote to Clement Attlee on what he called 'the grave constitutional issue' of the power of the Labour Party Executive, and especially of its Chairman, Professor Laski. Attlee wrote back to say that Professor Laski 'has not the power to give me instructions'.

That was an effective and straightforward way of dealing with the 'Laski Affair,' as it came to be called. But I think that Peter's way of dealing with it was far more effective than his leader's, though by no means as straightforward. It's true that he mentioned the professor by name on at least one occasion, when he said that 'Mr Churchill himself during the war had frequently consulted

Professor Laski. Now he reviles him'. But what Peter usually did was to make the Laski Affair irrelevant – or even dangerous for the Conservatives themselves – by claiming that his party and theirs had a great deal in common; especially when looked at from the perspective of a third presence that hovered over the 1945 Election – a genial one this time; not brooding like the others. This was Sir William Beveridge, who had given his name to a report that had been debated by the House of Commons in February, 1943. It recommended in outline the system of welfare and of social insurance that ought to be implemented by any government – whether Labour or Conservative – which came to power after the defeat of Germany. And both of these parties agreed to it, which enabled Peter to wonder at a public meeting 'why Commander Bell had not joined the Labour Party'. If their aim was the same, then the important question was not about keeping Mr Churchill or gagging Professor Laski, but about which party would be more effective at bringing into being the recommendations of the Beveridge Report – which included, of course, a Health Service that would be free for everyone. To clinch the matter, Peter was able to quote the Commander's claim that he supported 'a definite policy of full employment', and that 'immediate measures should be taken for the building of houses for the people'. This was all good Socialist stuff, previously unheard of from the mouths of Tory spokesmen, especially ones who called themselves 'Commander'.

And Peter was able to neutralise Professor Laski still further – by presenting himself to the people of Newport as a family man, while carefully avoiding any mention of the word 'divorce'. His son, David – now home on leave – and his daughter, Joan, made speeches for their father at a public meeting. David was wearing his army uniform on the occasion, which was evidence – if such were needed – that the Labour Party was by no means unpatriotic. He explained the increasing support for Labour in the armed forces by saying that they 'did not want to come back and suffer as their fathers had suffered after the last war'.

The present war was still continuing, of course, and not only in the Far East, where the Japanese had not yet surrendered; in all of the previously occupied countries of Europe, collaborators were being 'dealt with'. Women who had slept with German soldiers were subjected to the humiliation of having their hair shaved off as a temporary reminder of their everlasting shame. Other collaborators were being shot by members of the former Resistance – or by those with a personal grudge to settle – a danger that was faced by a sporting idol in France, the glamorous boxer, Georges Carpentier. During World War One he had been a hero, twice decorated by his own countrymen, which made him a celebrity in Britain as well. But later on, he was unsporting enough to take the European Heavyweight title from a British fighter, Bombardier Billy Wells, and he was also taking the girls by the score. So it was no more than he deserved when the *Illustrated London News* published a report, denouncing him as a collaborator with the enemies of his country – a traitor. The only trouble was, it wasn't the boxer, but some other Georges Carpentier: the *Illustrated London News* had failed to check its sources. The boxer's popularity – at any rate, amongst the girls – was to reach an altogether new dimension when he donated the proceeds of his libel action to a children's hospital – and one in Britain at that.

The affairs of Europe were being settled at a higher level – but with no less acrimony – at the Potsdam Conference on the outskirts of Berlin; where the British representatives were Mr Churchill and his Foreign Secretary, Anthony Eden. Clement Attlee went along with them as an observer, without official status. Churchill had sanctioned this in order that the Leader of the Opposition would know what was going on, and would be able to take over in the unlikely event of his winning the election, which was to take place while the Conference was still in session. The extra publicity gained by Mr Churchill from being a major figure at Potsdam was to be of benefit for Conservatives in the whole of Britain. In Newport, Commander Bell was to obtain a bonus on top of this. And at the best time possible.

The *Argus* for July 4th,1945 – the day before the election – reported him as saying that he had seen a statement by Mr Freeman in which 'he invites the electors to consider the lifetime of business experience his return would place at the disposal of Newport'. And then the Commander poured scorn on this claim, not with reference to the cigar factory – which had been successful by any standards at all – but with reference to one of the armaments factories that Peter had become involved with after abandoning his pacifism. 'Mr Freeman has been engaged in the manufacture of arms,' was how he actually put it, 'though I cannot say with profit'.

There was very little opportunity for an effective reply – just a single edition of the *Argus* on polling day itself, after a great many people had already voted, while others would do so on their way home from work, before so much as a glance at any paper at all. Nevertheless, Peter did his best. 'I am surprised that the *South Wales Argus* prints such a scandalous attack on me on the eve of the poll,' he said. 'My business record of 25 years as Managing Director of J. R. Freeman and Sons will, I believe, be sufficient justification to my claim to business experience'. And referring to the undeniable failure of an armaments firm he was involved with, he makes the point that 'All the other Directors were Conservatives'. Trust Peter to come up with that one – reflecting as much discredit on the Party of Commander Bell as on his own; probably more.

It was at a public meeting on the evening before Polling Day that Peter was subjected to a vicious anti-semitic attack, without being Jewish. This I discovered from a letter of protest by Mr A. J. Thomas that was published in the *Argus* immediately after Polling Day. It went as Follows:

'I was astounded to hear, while attending the Labour Rally, two youthful members of the audience ask Mr Freeman if he had always been known by that name, and, if so, was it ever spelt differently. For six terrible years the democracies have waged a bloody war against Fascism with its racial hatreds. Today in Newport, a small section of people still expound beliefs which we have sacrificed the cream of our nation's manhood to eradicate'.

Were these young people referring to the 'h' in Bernhard? Or to 'Freeman,' and wondering if it had ever been 'Friedman'? Either way, it looked as if they were trying to find something exotic in his name, something Yiddish, and either way it was nasty.

The poll took place on Thursday, July 5th, but the result was not announced until three weeks later, because of the time it took to collect the forces' vote, including the vote of those who were still on active service against the Japanese. On July 26th, it was announced in the *Argus* that Labour had swept to power 'in a sensational landslide'. And Peter was an MP once again, promising from the balcony of the Westgate Hotel – where Chartists had died for Democracy in1839 – that he would deal fairly with the problems of everyone in Newport, whether they had voted for him or not.

His party leader, Clement Attlee, had time to make only seven Cabinet appointments before returning hurriedly to Potsdam with his Foreign Secretary, Ernest Bevin. Their concern was to settle the affairs of Europe as quickly as possible. And this was Peter's concern as well, especially the affair with Eleonore Kastinger, a mysterious Viennese, which had been interrupted by the outbreak of war on September 3rd,1939, almost six years earlier.

Chapter 12

A Million Panes of Glass

IT MAY SEEM ODD – or perverse, even – to continue the story of Peter's long-postponed affair by giving you an account of a speech he made at the Newport Show for Gardeners and Allotment Holders. But it was on this homely occasion that he made his first public announcement of a forthcoming trip to Central Europe, including Vienna. And in the same speech he was to demonstrate – yet again – how far ahead he was in appreciating the dangers that mankind was having to face. On August 7th,1945 – some weeks before the Show – the *Argus* had carried a headline on its front page about a 'Colossal Blast Of A New Weapon' at a place called 'Biroshima' – a spelling mistake that would never again be made by any newspaper at all, anywhere in the world. Though it wasn't nuclear fission that Peter warned his audience about at that Show in Newport. He didn't need to, because Hiroshima had already become a synonym for destruction. He was more concerned to hammer home the message that a hungry world is a dangerous world, if less dramatically so than one with atomic weapons. And this is why – practical as ever – he had donated a Silver Cup to the Show as a prize for the growing of vegetables. He frequently argued that the gardens and allotments of Britain were helping to reduce our dependence on food from abroad, leaving more land available for the hungry people of the 'Third World' – though he wouldn't have used that term, since it didn't come into existence until after his death.

Peter exemplified, as much as anyone could, the genuine idealism of Clement Attlee's Labour Party. But there was another version of Socialism, too – that less benign one, already mentioned – whose adherents made a practice of tempting the politically innocent with a vision of Utopia, often by means of a joke or two. 'Joe For King' was chalked up everywhere in Britain, Joe being 'Uncle Joe' or Joseph Stalin, the High Priest of this other kind of Socialism. He was referred to in this affectionate way – and recommended as a replacement for George VI – because of being a wartime ally. His cosy image had been created by the portraits of him which appeared in the Press and on newsreels in the cinema, often with a little girl in his arms, but he was also responsible for the execution or imprisonment of unimaginable numbers of his fellow countrymen – many of whom had met their fate for espousing opinions that were no different from those of Peter – and amongst that number was the mother of the little girl with whom Stalin was so often and so charmingly portrayed.

Even nastier – perhaps a lot nastier – were those on the opposite extreme, like the man on trial at the Old Bailey in London. This was John Amery, accused of spending the war in Germany, attempting to form an army out of British prisoners-of-war – a so-called Legion of St George – that would fight for Hitler against 'Asiatic and Jewish bestiality'; for the holocaust, in other words. His father was Leo Amery – a Conservative MP – who had helped Churchill to power in 1940 by encouraging the Labour Party to support him in the House of Commons. John Amery was found guilty of 'adhering to the King's enemies in time of war', and was hanged at Wandsworth Prison on December 19th, 1945.

After reading about this and wondering what torments his parents must have gone through – imagining him with the noose around his neck, having once been their chirpy little boy – I went searching for some relief, as I often did at such a time, and I found it in an *Argus* report about a Newport soldier who was taken on a tour of Hitler's Chancellory in Berlin, 'where to his delight and astonishment he espied a copy of his local paper amongst the ruins'. The report doesn't mention whether some previous Newport soldier had left it there or whether Hitler himself might have taken the *Argus*, chuckling over reports of people on trial for bigamy, just like anyone else – which included a Newport woman sent to prison for being in possession of three husbands, not just two – all of them full of vigour – and who told the Court that she would 'do it again,' despite the impending sentence – or perhaps even because of it; prison would have provided her with a period of rest and recuperation before acquiring another three!

Those same idelogues of the extreme Left and extreme Right were competing on the Continent of Europe as well as in Britain, but for much higher stakes; nothing less than the subjugation of entire peoples. Communist revolutionaries were manoeuvring for advantage over the naive idealists of the democratic Left, while former Nazis were biding their time, hidden amongst the ranks of the respectable and democratic Right. It was into this sinister jungle that Peter went exploring in the autumn of 1945, and which he was to speak about at a public meeting on his return to Newport.

'There were scenes of almost indescribable desolation and misery,' the *Argus* reported him as saying, 'and there was rubble everywhere'. It was hard to imagine that he was talking about a part of Europe that had been renowned for its high civilization – an area of flamboyant architecture, of Mozart's music, and of a start to the scientific revolution, when a Polish monk was able to prove – contrary to common sense – that the earth went round the sun. 'The Russians had taken everything from the farms… hooliganism was rife… and a million panes of glass were needed for the windows of Vienna'. It was a moving performance that Peter gave – but not as moving as the reunion with Eleonore, which he didn't even mention. She had spent those years of separation in the top flat of an apartment block on the outskirts of the Austrian capital, waiting for him. They were ideally suited, both being adherents of Democratic Socialism and of Theosophy. She was also seventeen years his junior, a great advantage for retaining someone of Peter's undoubted ability in the arts of seduction. But she was no longer the woman that Peter had waved to from the window of his train, as it steamed out of her life in the late Summer of 1939. The block of flats where she lived had a basement in which the residents could take shelter during the bombing raids that were carried out towards the end of the war by the air forces of Great Britain and the United States. It also had a lift which could transport the residents away from danger down to the basement as soon as an air-raid warning was sounded. For some reason, Eleonore was slow in arriving at the lift on one such occasion. Her neighbours had already gone down, leaving the safety gates open in their panic. She tumbled into the shaft, landing on the roof of the lift, far below in the dark, and she never walked again. She could not sit up straight unaided, and was never free of pain. Peter married her at a Registry Office in the District of Wien-Hietzing as soon as he could make arrangements, which meant that Eleonore was legally entitled to go back with him to Britain, and to Penarth.

David Freeman – for all his sorrow at his father's disloyalty towards his mother – descrbed the wedding in Vienna as 'an act of great gallantry', which indeed it was. In fact, I would go much further, and say that Peter's second marriage was a long act of atonement for previous misdeeds – but one he accepted gladly.

He and Eleonore went to live at the house in Rectory Road, where an extension was built for an indoor swimming pool, so that Eleonore could exercise – the only time she ever left her wheelchair, apart from going to bed. So deftly was she incorporated into Peter's way of life that no-one seemed to realise there was a new Mrs Freeman as mistress of Rectory Road. Some of the Penarth Oral History Group claimed that the lady in a wheelchair was the first Mrs Freeman after a crippling attack of polio, a disease that was rife at the time. Peter referred to her as 'Ellie', which for all practical purposes was close enough to 'Ella' for the deception to be complete. Not that Peter hid her away, as did the families of so many other disabled people in those less enlightened days. On the contrary, he was very proud of her. She went with him to public meetings, a striking figure on the platform in her wheelchair and her hats, which were quite something, apparently. And as time went on – obliterating the distinction between her and the first Mrs Freeman – she would say a few words at those meetings, delighting everyone with the charm of her pronunciation and vocabulary. The point is, Peter was a politician with something to hide – by the standards of the times – which left him vulnerable to innuendo, publicly as well as privately. And although he took Ellie to a great many places, he didn't want any awkward questions about her, not if he could help it. So the fortunate similarity between 'Ellie' and 'Ella' was very useful to him, despite the ever-present danger of murmuring the wrong one in his sleep at night. Equally useful was the old address in Penarth, and the rumour about 'poor Mrs Freeman's attack of polio'. Peter's skill at integrating this new wife into his old routine was so effective that Ellie received an invitation to accompany him on a visit to Buckingham Palace, where she was presented to the King and Queen. Whether they were invited in spite of Peter's divorce, or because the royal bureaucracy was unaware of it, I'm unable to say, but I suspect the latter; when Peter died, there was a similar ignorance about the number of his marriages in the *Times* obituary, whose authors – I should imagine – are not chosen for their lack of inquisitiveness. All in all, it was a brilliant piece of camouflage.

While making notes about Ellie's visit to Buckingham Palace, I couldn't help thinking how delighted Ella would have been to receive an invitation there. Poor Ella! Instead of meeting the King and Queen, she had to endure those solicitous people in the street who gave her yet more examples of Peter's infidelity, always introduced with some vile little phrase – 'I thought it only fair' etc, etc. – which made it sound as if they were doing her a favour. She moved to Lane's End, within easy reach of London and the variety it could offer even in those very austere times, but far removed from all that really mattered to her – the friends she'd made in Wales, the committees she was on, and, of course, her beloved Guides.

Now that his home life was stable once again, Peter got on with the job of being an MP, and he did it superbly. Amongst all the changes that were taking place in the economy of South Wales – and of Newport in particular – he made sure that his constituents were treated fairly, especially as regards employment. It was obvious, for example, that the Royal Ordnance Factory would be going out of existence, as ammunition and explosives were no longer needed in such quantities. It was reborn as Standard Telephones and Cables, a major employer in Newport; with Peter acting as midwife, nagging the relevant minister in Parliament. The workforce were very lucky in their MP, because he was already an experienced politician, and Peter in his turn was lucky to be dealing with Sir Stafford Cripps, President of the Board of Trade and a Christian Socialist of the highest rectitude. As a Fellow of the Royal Society, he was a considerable scientist; and as a King's Counsel, he was a considerable lawyer. He seemed to know everything, and on top of it all, he was incorruptible, unbending, and – it must be said – unsmiling. 'There, but for the Grace of God, goes God!' was how Churchill put it, when Sir Stafford was a member of the wartime cabinet. But he was also on Peter's side in the matter of encouraging full employment, whatever their differences in other, more personal respects, which meant that the transformation from ROF to Standard Telephones and Cables went as smoothly as it possibly could, with a minimum of redundancies, most of whom were soon taken on by other firms in the locality.

Peter was equally fortunate in his dealings with other ministers – like George Strauss, who was responsible for government funding of the proposed Severn Bridge, so vital for the economy of Wales by cutting down on transport costs from England, and thus improving the compeitiveness of Newport Docks as an outlet for exports from the South West, from the London area, and from the Midlands. This Minister had been a champion of parliament at tennis from 1929 to 1931 in the Men's Doubles, with the

Member for Brecon and Radnor as his partner.

Peter was just as conscientious at dealing with his constituents on a more personal level, sending them letters of congratulation or of condolence, whenever there was a birth, a marriage or a death, and when they had a problem, he was as tenacious at dealing with it as any terrier with a rat, if his spirit – wherever it might be – will forgive me for that savage comparison.

One such problem was reported in the *Argus* on June 5th, 1947, and concerned the wife of a Newport soldier who had not yet been discharged from the army, even though the war had long been over. In the normal course of events, this soldier would have been entitled to a pass every now and again, allowing him to travel free on the railway for a visit to his wife. But he couldn't make use of this entitlement because he was confined to a sanatorium in Denbigh, North Wales, being treated for the tuberculosis which he had contracted while on active service. The passes were stopped, while his wife had to pay her fare to North Wales whenever she went to visit him. She was not well-off and had tried all ways to obtain some help with the cost of travel – applying, amongst other places, to Newport Council and to the Army – but everyone turned her down, there being 'nothing in the regulations' that allowed them to help this poor woman. Until, that is, she went to see Peter, who took the matter up immediately with the Secretary of State for War. Shortly afterwards, he received a letter from this minister, which was printed in the *Argus*:

'Dear Mr Freeman,' it said. 'You will be glad to know that arrangements have now been made to provide free travel for wives to visit soldiers undergoing long-term medical treatment... in place of the privilege leave warrants to which the soldier himself would normally have been entitled'.

Very satisfying indeed, because the problem had been solved not just for the Newport wife, but for all wives in a similar situation. It was even better than that, because the new regulation would apply to some other next-of-kin – to a mother, perhaps – if the soldier wasn't married. And it was almost entirely Peter's doing.

1947, the year in which this came about, was also the year of Indian Independence – something that Peter had been advocating for most of his life, since he first began to write letters for publication in his parish magazine. After his election at Brecon and Radnor, he questioned the relevant minister, Mr Wedgewood Benn, as we already know, and at Newport he spoke about it to all kinds of audiences, including his favourite kind, one composed entirely of women. This was at the Town Hall in 1946, when he summed up his argument by saying that 'In face of the problem of India, our pride in democracy is vainglorious'. Those women must have been impressed – and very much so – because apparently they 'clapped him to the echo'.

He loved the Indian people and was ideologically committed to their independence from Britain, but this didn't prevent him from dealing with a complaint that wasn't in accord with his ideology or his love.

'Why Are Our Nurses Left In India?' said an *Argus* headline of October, 1947, two months after independence had actually been achieved, and two years after the end of the war – which was more important, really, as these nurses were attached to the army. One of them – a Newport girl – is quoted as saying that they were 'forced' to nurse Indians injured in riots, and had been left without the 'protection of British troops'. Later on, she went even further, claiming that the nurses had all been treated 'disgustingly' by Indians.

Such a report must have been very upsetting for someone of Peter's inclinations, whether politically or theosophically. Nevertheless, he took it up in the House of Commons, wringing a promise from the Secretary of State for Commonwealth Relations that the nurses would be 'brought home as quickly as the available transport will allow'.

So what was there left for Peter to do, now that he was a husband once again and an active parliamentarian? Well, for one thing he could become a grandfather, which was achieved in November, 1945, thanks to his daughter, Joan. The announcement of this birth in the *Argus* had said that the baby was born at Aberystwyth, so I wrote to the local paper, the *Cambrian News*, asking for the baby – who would now be grown up, of course – or anyone else who might know of his whereabouts to get in touch with me.

It was an opportunity to find out more about Peter from his closest family, none of whom I had yet been able to contact – not even David – as I had no idea where they might be. The only Freeman I had spoken to was Nicholas, who had died with such panache in the Caribbean, but he couldn't tell me where Peter's son or daughter might be living. The weeks went by and then the months. Still no response from any readers of the *Cambrian News*. Not so much as a single, solitary word. So I began to wonder if my letter had made it into print. I rang up to ask – somewhat anxiously, I must admit, not wishing to appear conceited – and was told rather apologetically that it hadn't. 'But to make up for it,' they said, 'we'll do a feature about you instead'. And what a marvellous feature it was, referring to me as an 'author,' which I liked. Better still, it resulted in a letter from the father of that baby, Peter's son-in-law, Professor Thomas. He told me that he couldn't be of much help because his wife, Joan, had died, but he put me in touch with David and his wife, Ray – without whom this book would have been a mere academic exercise, a shadow, instead of a story with flesh and blood and feeling. And the baby? He is also a professor now – the one who told me about the games that Granny Ella used to play with him, making her fingers disappear.

Another cause for celebration in that post-war period was the ninety fifth birthday of Peter's mother in January, 1948. It was sixty three years since that 'Dreadful Year' when she had nursed her entire family back to health from diptheria, scarlet fever, typhoid and measles, had run a business, and bought a house. She was now living at St Ives in Cornwall with her daughter Dolly, who never married. According to an *Argus* reporter, 'Mrs Freeman takes a daily walk alone, keeps her own accounts, and writes to each of her 82 children, grandchildren, great-grandchildren and great-great grandchildren on their birthdays'.

All in all it was a time of great contentment for Peter, as well as achievement. But there was a threat to him, looming from within the constituency. Early in 1949, the Newport Conservative Association chose the man who would challenge him at the next election, which couldn't be too far away. He was a formidable challenger, too – intellectually gifted, already experienced in politics, and a Welsh international sportsman. He was very much like Peter, in other words, except for one thing – Conservative or not, he was working class.

Chapter 13

Up Before the Beak

THE PERSON APPOINTED to disturb this new-found tranquility of Peter's existence – at least politically – was a Mr Ivor Thomas, who had been the Labour MP for Keighley in Yorkshire before crossing the floor of the House of Commons, a move that transformed him into the Conservative MP for Keighley. He was a truly remarkable man, having obtained a first in Mathematics at Oxford, and then another first in Classics, despite the fact that he had never before studied Greek. For recreation, he indulged himself in cross-country running, a sport at which he represented Wales, the land of his birth, where his father had been a labourer at the Star Brickworks in Cwmbran. And to crown it all, he'd been a government minister for the colonies as well – because his abilities had been spotted early on by Clement Attlee.

It was bad enough that Peter – a life-long champion of the workers – should now be opposed by one of their sons. What made it worse was the support which this renegade was to receive from an organisation called the United Housewives Association of Newport, a group of women who seemed unnaturally impervious to Peter's formidable charm. Their complaints about him had begun in the previous year, 1948, when he had supported a Bill to suspend capital punishment for a trial period of five years. 'Newport United Housewives protest at proposed abolition of hanging,' said the *Argus* – 'chiefly on the grounds that the majority of murder victims are women and children'. This was an exceedingly powerful argument, and one that was generally held. So no-one was surprised when the Bill was defeated in the Lords, despite the enormous efforts of Lord Raglan – Peter's friend and political ally – whose great-great grandfather had ordered the Charge of the Light Brigade at Balaclava. In his speech of support for the Bill, Lord Raglan had made the point that in a civilised country even barbarians ought not to be treated barbarously.

A year later, the United Housewives were confirmed in their support of capital punishment – and Peter further discredited – when a Newport man was put on trial at Exeter in Devon for the murder of a fifteen-year-old girl, with whom he'd been having an affair. 'He put his hand around her throat and squeezed,' said the *Argus* report, 'and afterwards he tied his belt around her neck'. Then it quoted the man himself, speaking from the dock. 'I kissed her goodbye, but she did not know, because she was already dead'.

It must have been very depressing for Peter to read this report, but he plodded on regardless, dealing with constituency business. There was a meeting of allotment holders, where again he made the point that they were both helping Britain to cut down on imports of food, and helping poorer countries by making those imports available for them, and at lower prices. There were complaints to be made in the Commons about the long waiting list for spectacles in Newport. Best of all, there was an opportunity for a dig at the United Housewives over the question of analgesic equipment for reducing pain in childbirth. When they wrote to Peter to say how desperate the women of Newport were for such equipment, and why on earth wasn't he doing something about it, he was able to say that he already had done something, in a series of questions to Aneurin Bevan, Minister of Health – so why hadn't they checked their facts before posting their ridiculous letter – which, he noted, was dated April 1st, confirming their status as fools.

But it was only a dig, nothing more, because the Housewives were holding on to their advantage in the matter of capital punishment. Furthermore, both they and their new-found hero, Ivor Thomas, were able to enjoy another advantage amongst the ordinary, uncommited voters. This was over the question of nationalisation – the taking into public ownership of major industries like coal and steel – which made it appear that Britain under a Labour Government was becoming increasingly like Communist Russia, a state where everything was nationalised, including the corner shop, and which required the services of a secret police force – supplemented by a network of informers – to prevent rebellion. It had all been said before, of course, many, many times. But now there was something new in it, because the post-war euphoria about Russia was coming to an end, and Stalin was being seen for what he was: no uncle at all. 'Nationalisation – A Warning By Mr Ivor Thomas,' said an *Argus* headline in May, 1949. 'It was nothing but serfdom,' he claimed, 'and will soon extend to everybody'. Including, presumably, the man who kept your corner shop.

Ivor Thomas failed to mention that the Labour Party had no intention of extending nationalisation beyond a certain limited range; nor did he point out that when he attended the Labour Party Conference at Bournemouth in 1946, a resolution in favour of allowing the Communist Party to apply for affiliation was defeated by a majority so overwhelming that it never again became a serious issue. And he made no comment when Peter was helping to find jobs at Lysaght's, the Newport steelworks, for refugees from Poland, another Communist country.

In the atmosphere of those days – with stories abounding of Communist fellow travellers who were posing as good Labour men – it looked as if Mr Thomas was on to an electoral winner, especially as he could claim to be in possession of inside knowledge about the state of the Labour Party, having once been an important member himself; a protege of Mr Attlee, no less.

But there was a weakness in many of Mr Thomas's statements about these wider issues; a hint of which could be detected in his condemnation of strikes in the coal industry, as reported in the *Argus* in February, 1949. He was saying how odd it was that there should be so much trouble in the mines when Labour supporters were claiming that nationalisation would make for better industrial relations. Well, yes, but it was equally odd that someone with a first in Mathematics – and therefore in possession of a logical brain – should have failed to make a comparison with unrest in other industries that had not been nationalized: were they better, worse, or much the same? Ivor Thomas was not the first mathematician or logician to put ideology in front of reason, or to be swayed by his emotions. But the voters of Newport were not aware of this, and neither were Peter or his agent, Reg Ley. They certainly missed their chance when Mr Thomas gave his reasons for leaving the Labour Party. 'I saw the nightmare of an omnipotent state,' he declared, extending his argument from the nationalisation of particular industries to centralisation in general. Peter could have replied convincingly that he had already seen such a nightmare in Russia, and Reg Ley could have supported him by saying that he had seen its possibility also, as a UN Observer in Greece, and that neither of them could detect any signs of it in Mr Attlee's Britain. To clinch their argument, they could have asked Mr Thomas about the Polish couple who had arrived in Newport as stowaways aboard a ship, and had been granted asylum there. Would they have taken the risk of being found when the ship was searched in Gdansk – with the certainty of prison to follow – if Britain were heading towards the same kind of dictatorship as they were hoping to escape from? No, of course they wouldn't.

But none of this was put forcefully enough to Mr Thomas, either in the *Argus* or anywhere else.

Peter had the advantage – as a sitting member – of producing results for the people of Newport, something that was probably far more effective than all the arguments in the world. Especially when compared with the wilder accusations of Mr Thomas. Or his fan club in the Newport United Housewives. And Peter had a fan club, too – the women's sections of Newport Labour Party, who never allowed the 'Housewives' to forget how wrong they had been in the matter of analgesia for women in childbirth. Another advantage that Peter had amongst the women of Newport was Ellie. He was the devoted husband – not ashamed to take her out in her wheelchair, even to Buckingham Palace, and buying her those wonderful hats. 'Bless him!' they said. 'Isn't he marvellous!' It was partly because of Ellie that he had taken up another good cause, one that would earn him a maximum of Brownie Points from all sides. Because, unlike the abolition of capital punishment – or animal rights, if it comes to that – it was something that even the United Housewives were bound to agree with. He was pressing the Minister of Labour to establish a factory for the disabled at Newport, where they could make their own contribution to the economy.

And in any case, when it came to women, it must always be remembered that Peter was Peter; whether it was their vote he was after, or anything else. But even charm can have its disadvantages. Ivor Thomas made no mention of Peter's reputation as a ladies' man. And nor, to be fair, did anyone else in the Conservative Party. But there were powerful organisations that might well have done, given the chance. In December, 1949, the Lord's Day Observance Society had made an official complaint about an amateur pantomime – 'Puss in Boots' – that was to be performed in a works' canteen on a Sunday. The police might well have turned a blind eye to this illegal performance; some of them might even have taken their children to see it – but that was now impossible, absurd as it might seem. The Society was equally capable of attacking Peter – in public, too – because of his reputation as a Casanova, however much he might have changed. Together with their allies in the chapels, they might even have brought about his defeat at the forthcoming election, if it proved to be a close one. There was, however, another pantomime that year – apart from 'Puss in Boots' – which the Lord's Day Observance Society couldn't put a stop to. 'Newport Family Went Over Roofs In Nightclothes,' said the *Argus* headline. 'Busy Christmas For Fire Brigade'.

The Election was to take place in February, 1950, with the main issues being the predictable ones of nationalisation and centralisation. This suited Ivor Thomas down to the ground, since these were the very issues that had caused him to leave the Labour Party. At a mass meeting in Ninian Park, the Cardiff City Football

Ground, Mr Winston Churchill – Leader of the Conservative Opposition – said that 'The Welsh people must be careful in case the handcuffs of centralisation are clapped on them by a Socialist government in London'. When he had been on Paddington Station – about to board the train for Cardiff – Churchill was greeted by a sporting hero, Freddie Mills, the World Light Heavyweight Champion. 'Good luck, sir!' Freddie had shouted out to him. And Winston had replied with his trademark 'V–For–Victory' sign. Naturally, it was reported fully in the 'Argus,' leading to mutterings in Newport Labour Party that the encounter between these two great fighters had been arranged beforehand by Conservative Central Office. But whether it was or not, it certainly gave added weight – however unfairly – to Churchill's claim at Ninian Park that 'Socialism is a mental disease, happily not incurable'.

At a meeting in Newport, Peter dealt with the question of nationalisation by stating that Ivor Thomas had once been in favour of it, quoting him as claiming that the steel industry in paricular was 'too important to be left in private hands'. At the same meeting, Ellie supported her husband by saying that, 'Before my accident I travelled all over the world, and no country I have visited enjoys such good living conditions as Britain'. And by 'living conditions,' she meant things like freedom of speech and of religion, thus disposing of Churchill's jibe about centralisation and the metaphorical handcuffs it would bring. Reg followed her by saying that 'Mr Freeman had replied personally to more than forty thousand letters from constituents during the period he'd been a member of parliament,' making him a quite outstanding MP, perhaps the most outstanding of them all.

Unfortunately, the playgrounds of Newport failed to come up

with an electoral song in 1950, whether for Peter or for Ivor. The Labour Party did its best, though no political machine has ever been able to match the vigour or venom of children at school. The only verse I can take to in any way at all is this one:

> Do not trust the faithless Tories,
> Led by those who are turncoats.
> Full of lies and fancy stories,
> Do not let them get your votes.

Ivor's mournful predictions about the dangers of nationalisation and of centralisation couldn't possibly have had any effect whatsoever upon the people of Newport, because Peter won again, with an increased majority – which was all the more remarkable for the fact that Labour fell in Britain as a whole from 393 seats to 315, giving them a majority against the Conservatives of only 17. It was Reg Ley, as much as anyone, who had secured this triumph for Peter, by praising the work he had done in the constituency: for the disabled; for wives who could not afford to visit their sick husbands in the army; for nurses who were stranded in India; for everyone, in fact – including the Chamber of Commerce, which had thanked him for his support of local businessmen, most of whom would not have put their crosses against his name.

It was for this reason – I feel sure – that Ivor Thomas resigned his candidature and went to look for a more winnable seat, forcing the Newport Tories to go through the exhausting process of choosing a replacement. This was Lieutenant Colonel T. E. R. Rhys Roberts, a Welsh-speaking Londoner who had been the prize cadet at Sandhurst, and had since become a barrister in Cardiff, so he was by no means a pushover. But it was from his own side

– from Labour – that Peter had most to fear in the run-up to the next election, which couldn't be long delayed, given that slim majority in the Commons.

Early in July, 1950, Peter asked the Home Secretary 'whether, in view of the cruelty involved so far as animals and birds are concerned, and the frequent accidents to children, he could not consider taking steps to render the use of catapults illegal'. Naturally, there was much laughter when the Home Secretary replied that he did not think it would be appropriate 'to single out for prohibition this particular method of discharging missiles'. That laughter was only to be expected, since most of the honourable members would have been catapult owners themselves at some stage, and Peter must have laughed as much as anyone. But there was to be a supplementary question from another Mr Thomas – George, this time – the Labour MP for Cardiff West, who would later become a Speaker of the House. 'Will you take steps,' he asked, 'to see that all children hehave with the dignity and decorum of the Member for Newport?'

'I have often wondered, in considering his questions to me, how he did behave as a boy,' was the Home Secretary's reply.

This is a reply I find annoying, as I can't help feeling protective towards my subject, but nothing like as annoying as the question from Mr Thomas which had elicited that response. What right did Mr Thomas have to poke such fun at someone who had played games as a boy on a factory roof in London, putting his life in danger, and had captained his school at football, and whose adventurous son had spoken about him as a 'wonderful father' – whatever he might have been like as a husband. When Peter had been the MP for Brecon and Radnor, he used to ask David to fetch his car for him from the garage at the back of Rectory Road while he got ready for the trip to his constituency. It was a task that David enjoyed, because his father's car was a classic Chevrolet, which he loved to drive. And he did it regularly, without mishap, until he was spotted by a policeman – when it had to stop, because he could hardly see over the steering wheel, being only ten!

Peter was up before the beak – the magistrate – who awarded him the maximum fine, together with a lecture on the subject of parental responsibility.

No, Peter's fellow member – the future Lord Tonypandy – had no right at all to poke fun at him about his childhood. Especially when you consider that he'd never been near a football in his life – not with any boys of the rougher sort, or on a roof.

The next election was to take place a little sooner than expected, in October, 1951. Once again, the question of nationalisation was important, though not as important as another question, which paradoxically was something the Government and Opposition were agreed on. This was the question of re-armament against Communism, a political theory which Attlee had described at the TUC Conference in Brighton as 'a conspiracy against the liberty of common people' – reinforcing the Labour Party's traditional abhorrence of dictatorship, even a dictatorship of the Left – which, of course, was part of its inheritance from Chartism. But there were others who were not so sure. In April, 1951, Aneurin Bevan resigned from the Cabinet 'because the Government had decided to engage in an armaments programme which was inconsistent with the present standard of life and social services'. And he took a number of his colleagues with him, including Harold Wilson (who was to be the next Labour Prime Minister), all of them objecting to the sacrifices being asked for the cost of defending South Korea against the Communist North.

Peter remained faithful to Attlee, which made it easier for him with the voters in general; if not with the supporters of Aneurin Bevan, some of whom referred to him – somewhat inaccurately – as 'an establishment figure'. It might have been for this reason that Lt. Col. Rhys Roberts made a decision to ignore Peter and to concentrate his attention on the Bevanites, emphasising the fact that there was a split within the Labour Party. And what a split it was – an absolute gift for the Conservatives in every constituency, up and down the land. Wasn't Attlee forced to nationalise the steel industry against his own better judgement, merely to placate

Peter presenting a retirement gift to Reg Ley, his Newport agent, who had been both a pacifist and a general.

the supporters of his rival, the Honourable Member for Ebbw Vale? 'A vote for Socialism is more a vote for Bevan than for Attlee,' said Lt. Col. Rhys Roberts repeatedly, implying that Attlee would not be leader of his party much longer, but would be superseded by Aneurin Bevan, 'a wild man who wanted to nationalise everything' – which, declared the colonel, was obvious from the start, when you came to think of it, because he'd refused point blank to wear formal attire when summoned to Buckingham Palace on his appointment as Minister of Health.

At this election the Labour majority of 17 was to be replaced by a Conservative majority of 26 in the country as a whole. In Newport, Peter retained his seat comfortably, if not as convincingly as the time before. It's possible that Lieutant Colonel Rhys Roberts had made a tactical mistake by concentrating on Aneurin Bevan and the split in Labour. But what could he have done if he hadn't? Not a lot, really, because Peter was much too popular for him, and so was Ellie, with her wheelchair and her charming Viennese accent.

There was obviously a great deal of gloom throughout the entire Labour movement as a result of this defeat. They couldn't have been gloomier if their football team had lost. But comfort was at hand – just in time for Christmas – when the new Conservative Government was forced to announce a cut in the ration for bacon and for sweets. Sweets, mind you! Scrooge himself couldn't have done better.

Chapter 14

Up Before Another Beak

UNFORTUNATELY for Labour, these Scrooge-like tendencies didn't continue for long. Increasing prosperity – a world-wide phenomenon amongst the industrialised nations – enabled Mr Churchill to present himself as something resembling Father Christmas, especially when rationing was brought to an end within a year or so of our soldiers coming home from Korea in 1953, an armistice having been signed there. Newport Labour Party had its own paricular problems. The Conservatives had made some gains in the local elections, and Peter lost the services of his agent, Reg Ley, who decided to retire after working for him since 1935. But never mind. There was still a lot to be done.

He wrote a pamphlet called 'Animals And Men' in which he said that 'war, with all its abominations of atom and hydrogen bombs, cannot cease until Man puts a stop to his daily warfare on his younger brothers in the colossal barbarities of hunting, vivisection, the fur trade, and, most widespread of all, the common superstition that Man needs the flesh of animals for food'. Another pamphlet he wrote was 'Great Britain And The World's Food Supply,' using arguments that have become familiar to us all – partly because of Peter – but which in those days were strange enough to be considered eccentric, even ridiculous, because no-one had yet seen a famine on their television screen. 'We are faced with the threat of a catastrophe,' he wrote. And then he went on to give some figures he had obtained from the Ministry of Agriculture in London; a respectable source of information, if ever there was one. 'An average acre of land would produce about 168 pounds of beef in a year, but the same acre would produce 2,000 to 2,500 pounds of cereal or 20,000 pounds of potatoes'. So why are we producing meat, he wanted to know, when we could feed many more people by using the land for cereals or potatoes instead? 'Everybody who insists on eating meat is depriving about 50 other people of their food supply, somewhere in the world'. What, then, should the Government be doing? If they can't make vegetarianism compulsory – which he knew to be impossible – then they could at least discourage meat eating, while encouraging the growing of vegetables on allotments.

He brought the question up in parliament – in December, 1952 – when the Minister of Food had responded by saying that he hoped the Honourable Gentleman 'would not advocate the adoption in this country of a diet consisting solely of potatoes'. It was an utterly contemptible reply, which no minister – of whatever party – would get away with nowadays on the subject of famine, any more than the *Argus* could print a headline that said 'Gardeners Have a Chance To Be Gay' – which it did within months of that report, but years before 'gay' had ceased to be a synonym for 'cheerful'.

Earlier in 1952, he was part of a delegation that went to see the Minister of Supply about redundancies at the Aluminium Works on the edge of his constituency, these redundancies being caused by a lack of raw materials. Now, this minister was the roguish Mr Duncan Sandys, a womaniser of more than average competence, who might well have been described as the Tories' answer to

Peter Freeman – or, at any rate, to the Peter who had roamed both far and wide before his marriage to Ellie. Were the minister and the delegate aware of each other's reputations, I wonder? And if so, did they exchange a conspiratorial smile as their colleagues were holding forth? Because there must have been secretaries in attendance, female ones, both shapely and alluring. But it was certainly a friendly encounter, whether these two old heartbreakers knew about each other or not. And quite successful as far as Peter was concerned, with Mr Sandys 'intimating that he would make enquiries'.

The *Argus* report of this meeting would have been more than beneficial for Peter in the constituency, amongst the voters in general. But as we've said before – more than once, I believe – a politician must be especially careful about his natural supporters within the Party: those who knock at the doors, canvassing for votes and selling raffle tickets for election funds. This was a tricky problem for Peter at that time, as it was for every other Labour MP. The split between the moderate Mr Attlee and the radical Mr Bevan was, if anything, getting wider. And knowing this, the Conservative Agent had written to the *Argus*, craftily suggesting that Peter should tell the good people of Newport on whose side he was, and why. Well, he had no objection to telling the people in general, whether good or bad. What he didn't want to do was tell his own supporters, which he couldn't avoid doing if he told everyone else. He was bound to offend some of them, either the Bevanites or the Attlee people, and if he did that, he might dampen their ardour for arguing his case on those doorsteps, or for selling those tickets, or both. In his reply to that fiendish Tory agent, printed in the *Argus* on October 18th, 1952, Peter said that the split – 'so-called' – was the 'essence of Democracy', a reasonable difference of opinion between reasonable men and women. 'Unlike the Conservative Party, who are practically ruled by the personal decisions of one autocrat'.

Peter hadn't lost his touch as a games player – he'd forced his opponent into conceding an own goal.

1952 was also the year when King George VI died, while his successor, Queen Elizabeth II, was on holiday in Kenya. The *Argus* made its announcement on the front page in huge, black headlines – the biggest I've ever seen. In the report underneath, it said that a meeting of the Parliamentary Labour Party – with Peter in attendance – had broken up immediately on hearing the news, while the London Stock Exchange had closed down. A week or so earlier, the *Argus* had carried a headline on an inside page, saying 'Little Wendy Tried On Party Frock When Parents Were Out'. It was a much smaller headline than the one for King George VI – minute, in fact. And so was the report underneath, which simply said that Wendy's pride and joy – her party frock – had caught fire, burning her to death at nine years old.

Why do I mention this? Partly because I want to say that Peter would have written to Wendy's parents, regardless of how busy he might have been with making arrangements for attending the Royal funeral, but mainly because I want these words to be a memorial for Wendy, the only one she's likely to have.

'Let us snap our fingers at the moaners who tell us that Britain is finished,' said the *Argus* in its New Year's Editorial for 1953. 'We are a country where our beloved Queen and her Ministers can go to their people without armed escorts'. The *Argus* could also have said that Mr Attlee, Leader of the Opposition, went to the Commons every day by tube – the Underground – like any other worker. And when he was Prime Minister, living in Downing Street, he sometimes walked there, as Churchill did, while the war was on. Later that same January, the *Argus* reported that one of the very first people to receive a telegram from the new Queen on their hundredth birthday was Peter's mother. There was a photograph of her, too – still knitting.

In July, the Queen paid a visit to Newport as part of a nationwide tour in celebration of her recent coronation. And Peter – after meeting her – presented a commemorative plaque to Lord Street, which he considered to be the best decorated of all the streets in the town. In return, the residents of Lord Street presented Ellie with a bunch of flowers. Also Mrs Ley, Reg's wife, who was looking after Ellie by helping her to negotiate the curbs of Lord Street in her wheelchair. A week later, Peter was just as happy at a much more proletarian function. He was Guest of Honour at the Annual Dinner of the Newport Skittles League – containing many Labour voters, not to mention some marginal ones – where he presented prizes to the winners of the various competitions, including the Peter Freeman Cup, which he paid for out of his own pocket, as had been the case with the plaque at Lord Street.

The Coronation was as great a boost for Mr Churchill's government as a win by England's cricketers might have been – or her footballers – which is saying something. Add to this a spell of fine weather, and Peter had to be especially conscientious about keeping his name in the public eye. Not long after the skittles dinner, he is speaking forcefully in a Commons debate on the Severn Bridge Scheme, arguing that some definite action must be taken to 'ameliorate' the traffic problems between England and

Wales. 'It is pointless to plan the industrial and agricultural rehabilitation of an area and then to neglect the lines of communication without which that rehabilitation cannot function,' was how he put it, pleasing the businessmen of Newport as much as he had pleased the skittles players at their dinner.

But he was still the same old Peter, ready to espouse the most unpopular of causes, however uneasy he might be feeling about the possibility of a snap election. For the Tories might well have decided (and who could blame them?) to cash in on the credit they were being given for this 'New Elizabethan Age'. It was against the background of this governmental euphoria that Peter asked the Home Secretary 'to make it an offence for parents to beat their children'. And he received a very sharp 'No!' for his pains, as he would have done from the majority of voters, who probably assumed that such a law could mean imprisonment – or a stiffish fine at least – for administering the odd 'slap across the bottom' to a wilful offspring. Even most of the party activists would have been against him on this one, as had been the case with hunting at Brecon and Radnor.

No, it couldn't have done him much good either inside or outside the Party. And then, at the start of winter, just as he was 65, he was told that his mother had died, with the *Argus* making much of the fact that she had outlived nearly half of her children, four of whom had 'passed away in recent years'. Nothing makes you more aware of approaching death than the loss of brothers or sisters; beings you had once regarded as immortal, like yourself. The only good thing was that Arnold had survived, though they came across each other very rarely; at funerals, mostly.

But he still didn't sit around moping, not Peter! He was busy for the whole of 1954 – from January onwards – as a glance through the *Argus*, or the parliamentary reports in *Hansard*, would testify. One of these latter was given the title 'Initiative Test, Portsmouth (Cat)'. It was naughty of Peter to take up a problem for someone outside his own constituency, but you will understand why from the word enclosed in brackets. On November 24th, he asked the First Lord of the Admiralty 'whether his attention has been called to an initiative test instituted recently at Portsmouth whereby it was required to produce, inter alia, a cat and take it to HMS Vernon; and whether he is aware that a ginger cat was stolen from Michael Osborne, which has not been returned to him, and whether he will give instructions that no such tests involving the stealing of animals will be repeated'.

I couldn't tell you whether Mr Osborne had gone straight to Peter, ignoring his own MP, or whether his own MP had refused to take the matter up, or was ill; but whatever the cause, it's obvious that Peter had aquired a reputation as an animal lover – and a courageous one, too, considering the sneers he'd endured. The First Lord told him that 'an exercise to test initiative involved the search for a variety of objects, all of which were to be found on HMS Vernon. This was, however, misunderstood. The cat was returned within half an hour to the place where it was found, but unfortunately did not return to its owner. I much regret any distress that has been caused'.

Let's hope that it did return eventually. After running off to sulk – as cats will – unjustly blaming its owner for the inconvenience it had been put to.

There was a feeling in the air that 1955 would be Churchill's last year as Prime Minister, and that he would be succeeded by Sir Anthony Eden, who might then call an election to stamp his authority on the country, having for so long been living in the shadow of the Master. It was for this reason that the Newport Tories chose their candidate very early in the year, Lt. Col. Rhys Roberts having decided to concentrate on the law. Their new man was Mr Donald Box, a Cardiff stockbroker, who had no intention of allowing his opponent to 'see him off'; as had been the case with his immediate predecessors, all three of them. And with the Tories as favourites amongst the bookmakers, Mr Box was aided in his resolution by no less a person than Peter himself. In January, 1955, he decided to support a Private Member's Bill that would give a measure of independence to Wales; not much, but enough to annoy a great many people in the town, where only eight months earlier, the Scouts had paraded in honour of St. George, patron saint of England. The *Argus* reported the Chairman of the Constituency Labour Party as saying that 'Mr Freeman will have the opportunity to tell us his reasons for supporting the Bill', which sounds like a headmaster telling an unruly boy that he will deal with him later. This is one of the reasons why Peter decided to give such wholehearted support to Aneurin Bevan in his Commons Motion 'calling for discussions with Russia on Germany before all the countries concerned have ratified the German Re-armament Treaties'. The idea behind this re-armament was for Germany to share in the defence of Western Europe against a possible attack by Communist Russia. But any move to re-arm our recent enemy was regarded with suspicion – if not hostility –

by a great many people, especially in the Labour Party, where there was still some hope that the 'socialist experiment' in Russia could at last be made to succeed, now that Stalin, the cruel perverter of that experiment, had died.

In other words, Peter's support for Mr Bevan's motion would help to cancel out his support for the Welsh Home Rule Bill. It was – you might say – the excuse he'd thought up for the Constituency Chairman, the Headmaster. 'Please, sir, couldn't you let me off, sir? Just this once?' Though it must be said that he might well have supported the Motion anyway, judging by the pacifist nature of the articles he was writing in the 1950's on Third World Poverty and Animal Rights, which I've quoted from already.

Neither the Motion nor the Bill got anywhere at all; therefore, they didn't figure as major issues at the Election in May. So Peter was spared the trouble of having to answer awkward questions about them at public meetings, leaving him free to deal with his constituency record, which was good, and his record of support for the Severn Bridge, which was also good – and approved of by people outside as well as inside the Labour Party. What wasn't so good were the results at the local elections, which immediately preceded the national one. There were defeats for Labour at Newport – as elsewhere – including Reg Ley, who had remained on the council after retiring as Peter's agent.

Peter retained his seat, though his majority was cut by half; while Mr Box had received the highest Conservative vote since the days of Sir Reginald Clarry. It was all very depressing, especially as the Conservatives under Sir Anthony Eden had increased their majority at Westminster.

Of all the words that could possibly be associated with Peter, the most unlikely is the word 'grumpy'; which people used when telling me about the work they did for him during the election campaign of May,1955. And if he was grumpy with them – his supporters – what on earth must he have been like with his opponents? But grumpy or not – which meant tired or not – he would soon be fighting another battle that was every bit as important and emotionally draining as the election. This was nothing less than a battle for the soul of his beloved RSPCA against those who wanted to reach a compromise with the Research Defence Society over the question of using animals for experiments. The most important skirmish in this battle was a paper that Peter presented to the General Purposes Committee of the RSPCA in opposition to its Chairman, Lord Merthyr, who had agreed to consider an appeal from the Research Defence Society in the task of collecting as many as 10,000 stray dogs and cats per year for vivisection. In fairness to Lord Merthyr, it must be said that the Research Defence Society had given him an assurance that the animals would 'die a painless death'. But would they have enjoyed a painless or even a comfortable life before that? Peter was outraged, as you can imagine, but his paper was as cleverly argued as anything he'd ever done in his life, reminiscent of his article on decimalisation for the school magazine – despite the fact that he must have been working on it at the time of the election; with all the hustle and bustle which that entailed. He pointed out that collecting strays for research was illegal – a conclusion he had come to after consultations with the police and with lawyers – and that in any case it was totally opposed to the purposes for which the RSPCA had been established.

On July 7th, 1955, the General Purposes Committee decided by 7 votes to 2 that its Chairman, Lord Merthyr, should be instructed to discontinue any discussions he might be having with the Research Defence Committee, which made it a resounding victory for Peter, as it ought to have been.

But he wasn't 'himself'; not by any means.

And then – at a meeting of Newport Labour Party's General Committee in December, 'it was agreed that best wishes be conveyed to Peter Freeman, MP' – for a speedy recovery, that is. This was the first report I'd seen of Peter being ill since that attack of measles at the age of five.

1955 was ending badly, worse than 1954. But Peter was an avid reader of the *Argus*; and a story which would have caught his eye – as a former chairman of a fire brigade committee – was the one that said, 'Newport firemen made an attempt to revive a canary overcome by fumes. They took it out of a burning house and into the fresh air, and used an oxygen resuscitation set, but were unable to revive it.' Despite the sadness of that little tale, it would have warmed the cockles of Peter's heart, both as a lover of animals and as a champion of the working man.

'Mr Freeman Revolts – Quits In Protest,' was an *Argus* headline for April 21st, 1956. Peter had resigned his Treasurership of the Welsh Group of Labour MP's in a letter to its Secretary, Tudor Watkins – the Member for Brecon and Radnor – who had once been his agent. It had come about because of the Group's decision to oppose tolls for the Severn Bridge, whereas Peter had argued that, 'If 'no tolls' means 'no bridge', then we had better put up with tolls'.

He was still as logical and as much of a fighter as ever – to the end, in fact, of this particular incarnation – because on May 19th, 1956, he was up before another Beak, far from Penarth – but equally far from anywhere else – and one with a greater range of penalties than a mere fine, whether accommpanied by a lecture or not.

Cha pter 15

By Way of an Epilogue

AS SOON AS I received a photocopy of Peter's Death Certificate from the General Register Office in Southport, I took it round to Dr Redmore, my GP, who told me that multiple myeloma – which Peter had been suffering from – was a 'cancer of cells in the bone marrow, causing intense pain in the bones themselves'. When I told him that Peter had refused to be given morphine for it – on the grounds that it had been developed by experiments on helpless animals – he was as astonished as Nicholas had been, the nephew who got in touch with me when suffering from cancer himself.

This, of course, was the explanation for that 'grumpiness' which people had complained about at the time of the 1955 Election, and which was so unlike him. It was brought to light at his Memorial Service in the Methodist Church on Stow Hill in Newport, attended by a great many people including his children and his brother Arnold, though not by Ella, understandably. The *Argus* said there were 'gasps from a stilled congregation' when they were told about it by Peter's best friend in parliament, the MP for Baron's Court, Mr W. T. Williams. 'And Mrs Freeman nodded her head to confirm it was true'.

But what about the other Mrs Freeman? What about Ella? If Peter was right in believing that life is Karma – a series of reincarnations, with promotion or demotion on the evolutionary scale, according to one's conduct in a previous existence – then what could he expect? Would he go down to being a slug the next time round – a prey to hedgehogs and to gardeners – for the way he had treated his first wife? Or would he go up to being an angel for the way he had treated his second? The Karmic Accountant would have had a job on his hands with Peter, because what about those other women – the subject of so many hints, but whose names I was never given? And for the positive side of of that spiritual ledger, there was all the suffering he had gone through at the end. Where would that fit in – not forgetting the contempt he had endured on behalf of his fellow creatures, the animals.

Amongst the people at the Memorial Service was George Thomas, the future Mr Speaker and one of the most contemptuous. Did he have a pang of conscience, I wonder, when he heard about the morphine? Other mourners included James Callaghan, a future Labour Prime Minister, and the Chairman of Newport Conservative Association. But it was surprising how casually his death had been treated in the Commons a week or so earlier. Mr Speaker's tribute – if it can be called that – was reported in *Hansard* as follows: 'I regret to have to inform the House of the death of Peter Freeman, esquire, and I desire on behalf of the House to express our sense of the loss we have sustained and our sympathy with the relatives of the honourable member'. And then they went straight to the business of the day, beginning with a question for the Minister of Works about office accommodation in government departments.

There were tea and sandwiches and home-made cakes after the Memorial Service, which even the Chairman of Newport

Conservative Association couldn't resist, although they had been provided by the Labour Party. And there were no doubt stories, which people told each other as they balanced their sandwiches or their cakes on the rims of their saucers. I hope these stories included the one about setting off that fire alarm, and being chased by all those women at a railway station in Cardiff – quite a change from being the chaser – and buying roller skates for his employees; and wanting flowers in the House of Commons; and... And it's not the end of the story – at least, I hope not – because Peter is more important today than when he was alive, as a Green if not as a Casanova.

Titles already published

*For more information
about this innovative imprint,
contact Lefi Gruffudd at
lefi@ylolfa.com
or go to www.ylolfa.com/dinas.
A Dinas catalogue
is also available.*